"With this book, Mirra and Garcia remind us of the fundamental purpose of teaching and learning: building a world that is more compassionate, equitable, and free than the one in which we currently live. Their urgent call to action comes with a wealth of concrete strategies to help all educators begin to build the democracy of tomorrow alongside their students. This is the work of our time and this book provides the roadmap we need."

—**Ernest Morrell**, director, Notre Dame Center for Literacy Education, and Coyle Professor, departments of English and Africana studies, University of Notre Dame

"This beautifully written, much needed, and fresh vision of civic education will expand, if not transform, how civic educators pursue their goals. Mirra and Garcia detail educational principles that should guide civic education and they offer clear examples of innovative educational approaches consistent with these priorities. The book is a must-have for educators committed to helping students grapple with sizable problems in our society and work for a more just future."

—**Joseph Kahne**, Dutton Presidential Chair for Education Policy and Politics, University of California, Riverside

"What more beautiful gift could one offer to future generations than a (re)imagined education to help lift and restore equity within humanity? Drs. Mirra and Garcia provide a roadmap toward this goal in *Civics for the World to Come* while helping us see that teaching is a political act and all educators must be civic-minded practitioners toward teaching for social change. Civics education is the future of education and the framework provided in this book is exceptional, practical, and necessary."

—**Gholdy Muhammad**, associate professor of literacy, language, and culture, University of Illinois at Chicago, and author of *Unearthing Joy: A Guide to Culturally and Historically Responsive Teaching and Learning*

CIVICS FOR THE WORLD TO COME

NORTON BOOKS IN EDUCATION

CIVICS FOR THE WORLD TO COME

Committing to Democracy in Every Classroom

NICOLE MIRRA
ANTERO GARCIA

Norton Professional Books

An Imprint of W. W. Norton & Company
Celebrating a Century of Independent Publishing

Note to Readers: This book is intended as a general information resource for professionals practicing in the field of education. It is not a substitute for appropriate training. No technique or recommendation is guaranteed to be effective in all circumstances, and neither the publisher nor the author can guarantee the complete accuracy, efficacy, or appropriateness of any recommendation in every respect.

Some potentially identifying characteristics, including names, dialogue, and visual depictions, have been changed. Any URLs displayed in this book link or refer to websites that existed as of press time. The publisher is not responsible for, and should not be deemed to endorse or recommend, any website, app, or other content that it did not create. The author, also, is not responsible for any third-party material.

For information about permission to reproduce selections from this book, write to Permissions, W. W. Norton & Company, Inc., 500 Fifth Avenue, New York, NY 10110

For information about special discounts for bulk purchases, please contact W. W. Norton Special Sales at specialsales@wwnorton.com or 800-233-4830

Manufacturing by Lake Book Manufacturing
Production manager: Gwen Cullen

ISBN: 978-1-324-03021-8

W. W. Norton & Company, Inc., 500 Fifth Avenue, New York, NY 10110
www.wwnorton.com

W. W. Norton & Company Ltd., 15 Carlisle Street, London W1D 3BS

1 2 3 4 5 6 7 8 9 0

This book is dedicated to Dr. Ernest Morrell.
Our mentor, collaborator, and friend, you remind us to
love fiercely, fight like hell, and lead with hope.

Contents

Acknowledgments

This book represents a synthesis of lessons that we have learned in community with students, teachers, colleagues, mentors, and friends over a span of nearly 20 years. The list of those who deserve our thanks is endless. We acknowledge here just a fraction of those who have taught and learned with us, supported us, and pushed us forward in this joyful struggle. Thank you to all of our students—past, present, and future. Thank you to the members of the Council of Youth Research, the MS 50 Debate Team, the Digital Democratic Dialogue Project, and the Black Cloud. We are also grateful for support and mentorship from the National Council of Teacher of English, the National Writing Project, the Spencer Foundation, and the participants in the Speculative Education Colloquium. Thank you to everyone who offered feedback on the book in its early stages, especially Emma Gargroetzi and Mark Gomez. And thank you to Joey Luna and Stella Max for inspiring us to constantly seek more beautiful worlds on our horizons.

CIVICS FOR THE WORLD TO COME

Chapter 1

| | | | | | | | | | | | | | | | | | | |

Introduction: Imagining Pedagogies of Tomorrow

A t its core, education embodies humanity's hopes for the future. When you strip away the jargon of standards, strategies, and metrics, what remains is one generation's best attempts to prepare its children for tomorrows that—try as we might—we cannot accurately predict or control. As a society, we place our faith in educational institutions (primarily schools) to offer youth our best guess of the knowledge, skills, and dispositions they will need to live in a society filled with opportunities and challenges beyond our capacity to fully envision or comprehend.

One constant in these efforts is the desire for our children's future to be better than the present in which we currently live. While you the reader are encountering these words at a time after we the authors have written them, we imagine that several fundamental threats continue to loom over your present. The ripples of suffering and societal disruption caused by the global COVID-19 pandemic reveal the fragility of life and the shortcomings of our public health infrastructure. The fear and forced migration caused by war and climate disaster represent existential dangers to humanity and the planet. The continued scourge of racism perpetuates structural inequities and horrifying acts of hate and violence that presage the full unraveling of a social fabric that has always been tenuous at best.

The trouble, of course, is that while some consensus may exist about the ills of the present, we in the United States are bitterly divided about what a better future might look like. Many seek a society in which civil rights and the benefits of economic, social, and political opportunity are expanded to meaningfully include those who have historically experienced and continue to experience oppression according to race, gender, sexual orientation, country of origin, and other identities. Yet some instead seek to restrict opportunity and concentrate power to uphold the narrow ideological interests of groups seeking to exercise exclusionary and dominating power.

As portals to the future, schools have become the locus of intense contestation over who gets to define the better world of tomorrow and in turn what students should be taught in class to pave the way there. In raucous school board meetings, state legislative assemblies, and district planning sessions across the country, adults are seeking to control access to books and other instructional materials, mandate the topics teachers can discuss, and in some extreme cases restrict the categories of students who can fully access public education services.

These battles reveal the fallacy underlying one of the most common refrains repeated by those seeking to avoid controversy—that education is or should be objective. Attempts to control school curriculum demonstrate that every choice about content to include or exclude from classrooms represents the embrace of particular values. Attempts to control how teachers teach or how students express themselves represent specific ethical orientations. Attempts to adopt a both-sides approach to topics such as slavery and LGBTQIA+ rights imply, horrifically, that the identity and humanity of some of our students are topics for legitimate debate. This book argues that neutrality is an impossible and undesirable value to guide teaching and learning.

We acknowledge that this is a lot. Being or becoming a teacher today is a fraught endeavor considering both the blistering public scrutiny and the urgent stakes: no biggie, just the future of the world. As former K–12 teachers and current teacher educators ourselves, we know firsthand the pressures of this work, not to mention the frustration that comes with bearing such weighty responsibilities amid the consistent underfunding and undervaluing of our profession. While we understand the yearning that you may feel for a simple, step-by-step guide that can help you navigate these challenges with as little conflict as possible, we unfortunately cannot provide that. There is no sitting on the sidelines in teaching today; this is hard, complex work and one day soon you will be called upon to take a stand for your practice. What we can offer, however, is a resource to help you articulate your educational philosophy when that time comes, along with strategies for translating your commitments into rigorous, meaningful instruction with students.

More About Us

We began our careers as high school English Language Arts teachers on opposite ends of the country—Nicole in Brooklyn, New York, and Antero in Los Angeles, California. While we did not yet have the language of world-building in our vocabularies, we each embraced teaching philosophies focused on supporting our students to leverage the skills of academic disciplines (for us, literacy) to advocate for themselves and their communities in an often unjust world. We met as first-year doctoral students in UCLA's Urban Schooling program, where our shared experiences and commitments (and general pop culture obsessions) laid the foundation for professional collaboration and friendship that keeps chugging along—15 years and counting. We are grateful to learn from and work in deep relation with each other and the communities we describe in the chapters to come.

The ideas that we've explored together over the years and document in these pages have an intellectual lineage rooted in the research and praxis of artists and scholars from Black, Indigenous, and other communities of color—some of whom we've been fortunate to learn from directly as mentors, and some of whom we learn from indirectly through their work. Speculative thinking, expression, and practice emerges from these communities based on specific lived cultural and historical experiences, and we constantly humble ourselves as we engage with this work from our social positions as a white woman and mixed-race man. We cite them, honor them, and follow their lead.

Since we are asking a lot from you, it's time for us to lay our cards on the table. We have organized this book and our teaching practice around three decidedly non-neutral principles that we invite you to explore with us:

1. All teaching is political and all teachers are civics teachers.
2. Our teaching must demand just futures, not submit to the world as it is.
3. We can interrogate and innovate our teaching by embracing world-building commitments in the classroom.

We offer a brief introduction to each principle here and explain how the chapters to come will expand and deepen these ideas.

Principle 1: All Teaching Is Political and All Teachers Are Civics Teachers

It can feel scary, especially now, to openly declare teaching a political act. It feeds into paranoia about schools taking sides in ideological battles between Democrats and Republicans and contributes to instances of externally mandated or self-imposed censorship of ideas or curriculum. Yet rather than shy away from this declaration, we must carefully and forcefully disentangle the distinctions between politics and partisanship in education; instead of striving for a neutrality that has never existed and will never exist, we can identify values that we want to cultivate in our instruction to guide students toward the society of tomorrow.

Politics is not only about formal party establishments; more expansively, it refers to the complex web of relations among individuals living in community with each other (Wolff, 2016). Politics asks us to consider how we want to live together as a public. What do we value as a group? What competing interests exist within our collective? How should we make decisions that may affect various members of our community differently? Politics exist in every group, from families to nation-states and global alliances, and they overlap and intersect in various ways; the political values of countries influence those of families and vice versa.

From this perspective, the political nature of teaching and learning comes into clearer focus. As the public institutions to which we entrust the future well-being of our children, schools have always been trans-mitters of social values about everything from how we should treat each other interpersonally to how we should define success or progress as a nation. These values shift over time; for instance, while Thomas Jefferson and other founders of the country's public education system conceptualized school primarily as a vehicle for instilling democratic dispositions in the (white, male, and landowning) citizenry of a young and developing nation, the 20th and 21st centuries have seen the emer-gence of a range of priorities (Tyack & Cuban, 1995), from assimilation of immigrants into an American identity to national security and col-lege and global workforce readiness.

These macro-level values influence every aspect of schooling: district mission and vision statements, hiring practices, teaching philosophies, discipline policies, family-engagement plans, assessments, disciplinary curriculum, instructional strategies, and so on. Because these priorities often differ among community members at local levels, particularly when overlaid by the issues of power and structural inequity that have long riven U.S. society, schools become sites of intense clashes of values. Schools do not espouse Democratic or Republican perspectives; they express little-"p" political priorities that may get taken up by partisans to foment big-"P" political battles. This directionality makes a difference.

This is why we say neutrality is impossible in the classroom and there is no option of sitting on the sidelines. Even if we vowed to avoid all talk of the world beyond the four walls of our classrooms and follow our district's mandated curriculum to the letter, we would through these acts still be expressing political values. Thus, rather than ceding our pro-fessional expertise and allowing our practice to be wielded as a political football by others, we suggest that clarifying the values of our instruc-tion for ourselves can give intention to our work and help us navigate the contentious landscape of schooling today with clarity and purpose.

Understanding that our instruction implicitly and explicitly trans-mits messages about what we could or should value as a society leads to the latter half of our first principle: all teachers are civics teachers. This claim may seem jarring at first since content standards across all 50 states define civics as a bounded discipline concerned with the structures, policies, and procedures of the U.S. government and big-P political system and also locates this discipline narrowly within the social studies (Shapiro & Brown, 2018). In most school districts, there is a clear delineation between those who are identified as civics teachers and those who are not.

Again, just as we can expand politics to include not only formal partisan parties but also broader negotiations of shared public values, so can we expand civics to include not only formal government structures but also broader negotiations of community engagement. Civics in our interpretation is the study and practice of negotiating values in order to determine how to live productively and compassionately in relation with each other. Based upon this interpretation and the aforementioned positioning of schools as portals to the future, every teacher regardless of discipline is engaging in this negotiation with students each day in the classroom.

As we will discuss throughout the book, academic instruction—from the content and skills of each discipline to the pedagogies used to teach that content and the relationships fostered within and beyond each classroom—communicates to students potential pathways for civic life in the present and the future. The central question we ask you to consider is:

> *What vision of civic life are you communicating through your teaching?*

Put another way, to what do you assign value in your classroom, through grades or otherwise? Obedience? Creativity? Factual knowledge? Interpretation? Criticality? Cultural expression? You likely embrace multiple values at once, including inevitably some that live in conflict with each other. As you move throughout this text, we will continuously ask you to interrogate the vision of civic life built through those values. Is this vision one you think resonates with your students? How do you know?

Again, dispensing with the illusion of neutrality, we write to advocate a particular vision of civic life, one we explore in our second principle.

Principle 2: Our Teaching Must Demand Just Futures, Not Submit to the World as It Is

When we reflect on the aforementioned challenges stalking our students today we cannot help but fear for their future. In the midst of suffering and uncertainty, we cast our minds forward and wonder what their world will look like in 20, 30, or 40 years. We ask ourselves: Is what we are teaching them in our classrooms preparing them to build a more peaceful, healthy, and compassionate society than the one in which we currently live? Or are we just treading water and hoping that teaching yesterday's knowledge and skills will be relevant tomorrow?

We suggest that in too many classrooms today, instruction is indeed inadequate to support students in building just futures. With the broadest possible strokes that we will flesh out in the chapters to come, we sketch just futures as those in which racial, cultural, gender, and other identities are honored in all civic institutions, bodily autonomy is respected, more than human environments are protected and cherished, and decisions about public resources are designed to redress historical inequities and ensure the flourishing of all communities.

Why are we falling short? What would it take to get there? To be fair, we do not have much of a blueprint to follow. We have literally never lived in such a world. If we are being honest with ourselves, it is difficult to get specific about the exact policies, arrangements, and contours of a desired future that is so far beyond any reality we have experienced. Thus, we argue that one of the greatest challenges facing the field of education today is a failure of imagination.

Let us tell a short story to offer a fuller explanation. Back in 2019, the Brooklyn Academy of Music held an event featuring a conversation between racial justice activist and author Ijeoma Oluo and speculative fiction writer N. K. Jemisin. The focus of the talk was the relationship between activism and art. Jemisin writes in an artistic genre that has come to be known as speculative fiction in which authors—particularly authors from communities marginalized in public life—challenge oppressive and inequitable structures of the present by constructing fantastical futures in which those inequities are disrupted or absent. Oluo told Jemisin that she was inspired by the narrative worlds she created because they reminded her of the creativity needed in struggles for social change. She said:

> *I've always felt that activism is a very creative practice and where we fall short and where we're most threatened is the limits of our imagination. And especially I think for racial activism in a white supremacist world our imagination is so boxed in by white supremacy that our definition of freedom is even boxed in by white supremacy. What I'm constantly worrying and fighting against is the limitations—sometimes it's generational and sometimes it's not—of what we can imagine in the future . . . . Because I'm constantly telling people, like, I know that I don't know what freedom looks like. And my grandkids one day are gonna say, why didn't you see this? Why did you stop us here when we could have done more? I'm excited about that day when someone introduces a new possible future to me.* (Brooklyn Academy of Music, 2019)

Sitting in the audience that evening, I (Nicole Mirra) could not help but draw parallels between activism and education and the limits imposed upon our imaginations as teachers and learners by a school system built upon logics of social stratification and standardization. I kept turning that phrase over in my mind: "I know that I don't know what freedom looks like."

How can we teach toward a world beyond the one we have been socialized to accept—a world that does not yet exist? Yet at the same time, how can we not do so, when our students desperately need us to act in response to the existential threats they face?

These questions brought us back to the idea of civics. To us, the current paradigm of civic education is inadequate not only because it tricks many teachers into thinking that it is not their domain or responsibility, but also because it is philosophically designed to promote trust in and engagement with the broken institutions in the world as it is rather than encourage dreaming and building toward the world as it could be. The Civics Framework created by the National Assessment of Educational Progress (NAEP, 2014), which influences the standards and curriculum used across the country, is grounded in the belief that the country is on a steady march forward toward fulfillment of its founding ideals and teaches students to participate in formal democratic structures such as voting to continue this incremental process.

Such a belief rings a bit hollow when young people witness inaction, stalemate, or full backtracking in relation to the major social issues they face. Our young people see school shootings and other instances of gun violence happen with horrifying regularity. Meanwhile, legislative bodies fail to pass measures that the majority of voters want. Students see a rising tide of hate speech as states seek to forbid discussions—let alone action upon—continuing histories of systemic racism. They see worsening storms, droughts, and other indicators of accelerating climate change while mitigation efforts falter. Such a record does not inspire faith in the capacity or will of our existing civic institutions to do much to secure them a more just future. Public health officials have warned of an increasingly urgent adolescent mental health crisis; while various individual culprits are proposed (e.g., the pandemic, social media), young people are crying out to us about a collective despair at the most existential level regarding their future prospects.

We write this book because we cannot in good conscience continue working toward the goal of integrating our students into a civic life that is failing them. In order to maintain hope for their futures, we advocate for a reimagining of civic education—one that takes place in every classroom in every subject area at every grade level through every unit—that is committed to teaching students the knowledge, skills, and dispositions to build new worlds. We return to the lessons of speculative fiction to advocate a speculative civic education that centers the building of new kinds of public relationships rather than adherence to formal institutions and that cultivates joyful and intentional collective praxis toward new realities (as we described in Mirra & Garcia, 2022).

Again, we acknowledge that this work is difficult. It requires us to question and revise many of the assumptions about education, society, and ourselves as educators that we have been socialized to believe. The journey to begin discovering what freedom can look like is long and arduous, but it can begin today through the nurturing of new commitments to guide our practice.

Principle 3: We Can Interrogate and Innovate Our Teaching by Embracing World-Building Commitments in the Classroom

As we've discussed, the aims of civic education are often framed in terms of participation in and engagement with existing structures. We suggest that a more productive framing is interrogation of what exists and innovation toward new possibilities (as we first called for in Mirra & Garcia, 2017). Interrogating our teaching practice involves questioning the lessons, readings, and assignments that we offer our students, as well as the instructional strategies and relationships that we forge, to uncover the values and worldviews that they implicitly and explicitly espouse. Innovating our teaching practice involves making changes to our current repertoire and designing new learning opportunities that embody the knowledge, skills, and dispositions needed to construct better futures.

It is impossible to create a checklist of such knowledge since it will differ across disciplines and learning contexts and because it needs to emerge through collaborative partnership with students and communities. However, we have identified five practices that have emerged as powerful and promising through our work with learners across the country.

Our framework for world-building civic education (see Figure 1.1) starts with two overarching beliefs: first, that education is a tool that must be used to design new futures and second, that young people are experts in their communities who can use their voices to create equitable social change. Without deep investments in these two beliefs as a starting point for pedagogical practice, any attempts to engage with world-building concepts are missing their fulcrum. This is why "Equity & Justice" and "Youth Agency" in Figure 1.1 encircle all other commitments.

We have organized the rest of this book to delve into the theory and practice of this framework so that educators in formal and informal learning environments can apply it to their contexts and use it to inform their work with young people. Chapter 2 delves into the scholarship in educational research from which this approach emerged in

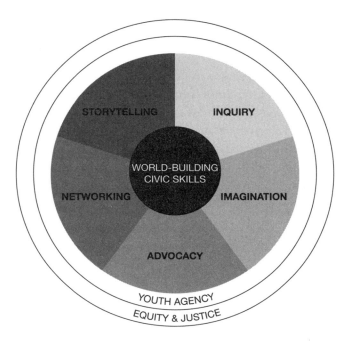

Figure 1.1   Framework for World-Building Civic Education

order to provide grounding in the ideological history that has brought our field to an embrace of the speculative. We review theories of learning that put equity at the core of young people's development and we summarize research in critical literacy, culturally sustaining pedagogy, critical race theory, and participatory design that informs our speculative conceptualizations of equity, justice, and agency.

The next set of chapters explore each of the five classroom commitments that make up our model of world-building civic education. Each chapter is structured to offer an introduction to the commitment, an overview of the barriers that our current educational system erects to its full realization in schools, and concrete strategies for interrogating and innovating classroom practice across disciplines drawn from our work with various learning communities from around the country.

We introduce the commitments here:

Inquiry: Supporting Students to Ask the Big Questions

Chapter 3 explores how the act of asking big questions about society is foundational to youth agency and the development of more equitable futures. Instead of continuing to offer assignments in which the only person who poses questions (or hears students' questions and answers) is the teacher, we discuss ways for educators to interrogate their own curriculum through the principles of youth participatory action research and critical pedagogy to elevate students as experts and knowledge producers in their own right. We share tools to help students ask questions that go beyond the boundaries of the academic and into the realm of the civic as the foundation for authentic community-engaged research projects.

Storytelling: Supporting Students to Listen and Tell Their Stories

Too often, civic education begins with giving students long lists of dates and facts and teaching them the structures of democracy within which they have to operate. Chapter 4 flips civics on its head by starting with youth stories about the communities they belong to and the type of society in which they want to live. Drawing upon the inspiration of critical race counter-narratives, we expand the range of civic texts beyond news articles to include stories in a range of different genres and modalities: fiction, art, popular culture, and beyond. We build upon Chapter 3's exploration of inquiry by demonstrating that before students begin to gather their own data about the questions that interest them, they need to learn the stories of the various stakeholders involved and see the personal in the political.

Networking: Supporting Students to Learn From Others Across Difference

We use the term "networking" to refer to both the interpersonal connections that students make with peers and adults as they engage in community inquiry and the digital media tools that structure many of these connections. Civic education and engagement look different in a digital world. Chapter 5 helps teachers think about the affordances and constraints of technology when it comes to participating in public life. Instead of focusing on technology as only a source of risk, we frame digital citizenship as a productive and interactive process. We share the stories of teachers and young people from around the country who use digital media to tell their stories across time and space in order to gain more empathetic perspectives and dream together about the kinds of futures they want for themselves and the wider community.

Imagination: Supporting Students to Play and Dream About the Future

While challenging social inequities is very serious business, it can be done in ways that forefront joy, play, and imagination. Chapter 6 pulls lessons from one of young people's popular interests—games— to explore the many creative ways that students can express what they learn from their inquiries with the world. Civic learning does not only have to take the form of PowerPoints or reports; students can design games for others to play, create imaginative forms of art and theater, and beyond. We share the stories of students and teachers who have channeled dreams for society into powerful examples of critical literacy.

Advocacy: Supporting Students to Make Their Dreams a Reality

Chapter 7 reminds us that schools are connected to rather than separate from the communities around them. As a result, student civic learning and engagement should be celebrated in the streets of neighborhoods just as much as on the bulletin boards of the classroom. If student learning is confined to academic outlets, it will not reach its civic purpose. Thus, this chapter focuses on avenues for students to communicate the results of their inquiry to various stakeholders in order to create change. We share strategies to help students and teachers develop marching orders for different groups—youth, teachers, administrators, families, elected officials, and beyond—and highlight the voices of youth whose advocacy for small changes built into lifelong commitments to civic engagement.

Put another way, these world-building commitments will support youth and educators to ask:

- Why are things this way?
- Whose stories need to be heard?
- How can we connect with each other?
- What kind of future do we want to build together?
- How do we get there?

We include discussion questions at the conclusion of each chapter geared at helping you and your colleagues clarify how each of the commitments can be applied in your practice. These interpretations are important to document and return to as a touchstone during the planning process.

Chapter 8 presents a planning template and resources inspired by the commitments and designed to catalyze the development of world-building lessons, units, and projects. We envision intergenerational teams of teachers, students, community members, and administrators using this template to spark dialogue about their dreams for the future and translate those dreams into new educational possibilities. The template is accompanied by testimonies from practicing teachers to demonstrate how educators take up these commitments in ways uniquely their own.

The element of this book in which we take the most pride is the amplification of the work of educators and youth who are close to our hearts. As you move through the text, you will encounter vignettes focused on the experiences of four specific learning communities we have worked with over the years who bring the various world-building commitments to life in transformative ways. Your understanding of these communities will deepen as you move through the vignettes; our goal is that you will come to know them and be inspired by them just as we are. Importantly, each of these communities engage in their work in hybrid spaces, by which we mean that some elements take place during the traditional school day in the context of formal academic instruction and others take place in the more informal space of after-school or out-of-school learning. This is no coincidence; we find that stepping outside the routines and constraints of school allows creativity to blossom in the design of learning. We strive to tease out the strategic moves we can make to infuse such creativity back into the classroom. Here is a brief introduction to our four focus communities, presented in the order in which you'll meet them in the chapters to come:

Middle School 50 Debate Team.   Debate is often considered one of the best practices of civic education and literacy education more broadly because it provides a format and structure to introduce young people to the nature of civic dialogue about issues of public concern. You can probably visualize it in your mind: students standing at lecterns persuasively arguing the merits of opposing viewpoints. The MS 50 debate team will turn what you think you know about debate on its head. This group of 6th-, 7th-, and 8th-graders from Brooklyn, New York, guided by their teachers and principal, turned a policy debate topic about immigration into an opportunity for all of us to reimagine how we talk about deeply personal public issues affecting the lives of our families and classmates. Their story also highlights the roles that inquiry, storytelling, and imagination can play in helping youth advocate for more compassionate and inclusive futures.

UCLA Council of Youth Research.   What counts as research? Who conducts research? When, where, and why does it happen? The high school students from South and East Los Angeles who comprised the UCLA Council of Youth Research offered answers to these questions that differed drastically from those that we largely find in classroom settings. Guided by their teachers and university researchers, these young people insisted upon exploring questions of their own choosing—questions that addressed social issues of authentic concern to them and their communities and that drew upon their expertise as organic civic leaders. Never content to blindly trust data from outside so-called experts who sought to spin deficit narratives about them and their schools, students developed their own forms of data collection that honored the stories of their peers, teachers, and elders. They also shared the findings from their inquiries with public audiences in order to advocate for educational transformation and social justice.

Digital Democratic Dialogue (3D) Project.   As more and more of our political discourse originates on and is disseminated through digital communication platforms, schools have begun turning their attention to digital literacy education. While such curricula often focus narrowly on teaching students to mitigate the risks of cyberbullying and misinformation, the teachers and students of the 3D Project asked what the affordances of social media might be for connecting students across time and space. In doing so, they found that they could share stories of their communities, discuss their developing perspectives on sensitive political issues, and dream of the civic futures in which they hoped to live together. This community linked schools from six geographically and ideologically diverse locations across the United States from the states of Alaska, California, Colorado, Michigan, Pennsylvania, and Texas in order to surface both the differences across our democratic lives and the commonalities that could form the basis for more a more humanizing public sphere.

The Black Cloud.   An alternate reality game that unfolded as part of the 12th-grade English curriculum in Antero's classroom, the Black Cloud was a cocreated experience merging data, citizen science, and storytelling. Working from the fictional premise that the pollution in Los Angeles has gotten so bad that it has developed a consciousness, students communicated with the titular Black Cloud while also measuring local air quality with custom-built sensors hidden throughout the South Central Los Angeles community. Students designed strategies for sustainable development and conservation. Combining scientific data with human experiences, students collaborated, shared, and analyzed their findings. In the game's final stage, students teamed up and created models of their ideal cities—their ecotopias—made out of locally sourced and found materials.

The book concludes with a call to action for all adults to find entry points to partner with youth to codesign the education (and the futures) that they deserve. Rather than tinkering around the edges of our broken democracy through incremental changes, we reiterate the need to respond to the youth-led movements calling for the dismantling of inequitable social structures with the construction of the new world to come.

Chapter 2

|||||||||||||||||||||

The World-Building Approach: Theorizing Our Commitments for Practice

In the first chapter we introduced the idea that every choice we make as teachers in the classroom reflects political values. One of the reasons identifying the political in our practice can be so difficult to do is that many of the resources offered to guide our thinking about our professional development adopt a functional and utilitarian approach: *"Five tips for effective writing instruction." "A step-by-step guide for classroom discussions."* Of course, there is a reason for the ubiquity of such streamlined, strenuously neutral-sounding support. Teachers are asked to do too much with too little for too many students at a time and the search is always on for strategies that can be distributed and scaled easily. While we understand that we cannot spend too long at the 20,000-foot level when we have lessons to prepare on the ground for tomorrow, we do believe that there is something crucially important about taking a step back from the grind to consider the ideas and beliefs that explicitly and implicitly inform teaching and learning. Theory informs practice, and spending a bit of time with our heads in the clouds is all the better for helping us dream of tomorrow's pedagogies.

Thus, we dedicate this chapter to a deep dive into the theoretical concepts that inform our approach to world-building civic education. In order to imagine what equitable futures could look like for our society, we must reconsider the dominant assumptions about civic life and civic education that we have been socialized to take for granted as educators. We also must recast our thinking about who young people are and what they are capable of bringing to a renewed civic life. In order to do this, we synthesize thinking from visionary scholars across the fields of political science, literary and cultural studies, and education that help us to understand the intersections of democracy, race, and literacy and articulate new pathways for civic learning.

Slowing down for theory can help us clarify our teaching philosophies and determine what we want to eliminate from, change, and add to our instructional repertoires. Our hope is that you can return to these ideas periodically as a gut check for your work, much as we do, and continuously recalibrate your efforts to educate toward justice. Our first task is to clarify our use of the "civic" in civic education.

Defining the Civic

Citizenship is an inherently fraught concept considering continued attempts to legislate, both in courts and in public opinion, the categories of human beings who can lay claim to civil rights and responsibilities and enjoy full inclusion in this country. In our conceptualization of civic life and of young people as developing citizens throughout this book, we reject narrow legal definitions that attempt to create binaries that "other" and dehumanize any individuals living in this nation. Our understanding of the civic instead hinges on ideas of democratic community as understood by activists like Ella Baker (as profiled in Ransby, 2005): one that is not limited by the formal communities of local, state, and national politics but expansively includes the informal communities of fellow citizens united by shared interests and concerns. We hearken back to John Dewey's (1916) understanding of democracy as not only a system of representative government, but also "a form of associated living" (p. 16). From this perspective, civic engagement includes explicitly political acts such as voting but also behaviors representative of what political philosopher Harry Boyte (2003) calls a "different" kind of politics, one that "builds the commonwealth" between individuals of various backgrounds, experiences, and beliefs by being "productive and generative, not simply a bitter distributive struggle over scarce resources" (p. 9). In turn, civic education involves the processes through which young people gain knowledge, skills, and identities they use to understand and participate in these forms of community life. These processes, particularly in school settings. reflect contested understandings of community that we need to excavate.

Brightly Rendered vs. the Murky: (Re) Interpreting Our Civic Life

This is the foundation of the [American] Dream—its adherents must not just believe in it but believe that it is just, believe that their possession of the Dream is the natural result of grit, honor, and good works. There is some passing acknowledgement of the bad old days, which, by the way, were not so bad as to have any ongoing effect on our present. The mettle that it takes to look away from the horror of our prison system, from police forces transformed into armies, from the long war against the black body, is not forged overnight. This is the practiced habit of jabbing out one's eyes and forgetting the work of one's hands. To acknowledge these horrors means turning away from the brightly rendered version of your country as it has always declared itself and turning toward something murkier and unknown. It is still too difficult for most Americans to do this.

—Ta-Nehisi Coates,
Between the World and Me (pp. 98–99)

From the perspective of African American writer and journalist Ta-Nehisi Coates, the American Dream represents more than simply economic opportunity or material success; it also signifies a fundamental belief in the virtue of this country. According to the Dream, the American narrative is one of triumphant progress, and any behavior contrary to this ideal, including oppression, brutality, or hate, is a mere aberration from American character rather than a manifestation of it.

The Dream is powerful; indeed, much of the formal education provided to U.S. youth about what it means to be a citizen is built upon its vision. Many state civic learning standards focus "almost exclusively on patriotic observances" (Torney-Purta & Vermeer, 2006, p. 16) and students are more than twice as likely to study heroes and U.S. civic virtue in their social studies and civic courses than problems facing the country (Vickery, 2017).

Consider again the National Assessment of Educational Progress (NAEP) in Civics introduced in Chapter 1, the most comprehensive and influential measure of civic knowledge and skills in the nation. In the framework for the 2014 exam, the governing board lays out a specific vision for how students should be taught to see their nation that fits strikingly well into the vision Coates critiques. They make passing reference to the bad old days when we experienced a "gap between the nation's ideals and reality" but highlight the progress Americans have made to "abolish slavery" and "remove legal support for segregation," concluding with glowing praise for "Americans [who] have joined forces to work toward the achievement of their shared ideals" (p. 19).

Thus, much of the civic education young people experience in school encourages them to engage in public life based on the core assumption that the infrastructure of our democracy is sound, that all citizens enjoy equitable access to opportunity and can use the tools of self-governance to remedy any threats to such opportunity. Our schools largely educate toward the Dream.

For those, like Coates, who see the agency of their communities stripped away by systemic inequities in multiple areas of public life, including criminal justice, law enforcement, and education, citizenship is a much more fraught proposition. The lived experiences of many people of color and those from other marginalized identity groups contradict the inherent logic of the Dream; as a result, these citizens must continuously negotiate the extent of their identification and engagement with a society in which they have experienced the "horrors" named by Coates—a painful process that W. E. B. Du Bois (1903) described over a century ago as the struggle of "double-consciousness" (p. 5). Institutionalized racism remains the uniquely American foundational tragedy that shapes citizenship. In his book, *In a Shade of Blue: Pragmatism and the Politics of Black America*, Eddie Glaude (2007) argues that "our reflections on democracy in the United States must begin by engaging the historical legacies of racism that threaten democracy's realization" (p. 40). He echoes the ideas of critical race theorists such as Crenshaw and colleagues (1995), who deconstruct how narratives of objectivity and meritocracy in American life serve to structurally privilege whiteness and white supremacy and perpetuate inequity.

In contrast to the normative framing of civic life expressed through educational policy documents like the NAEP framework, a vision of civic education informed by critical race theory must question whom civic education benefits, from what stance it educates, and how it renders American identity. As developmental psychologists like Watts and Flanagan (2007) suggest, the traditional framework can be fundamentally alienating for young people from minoritized communities whose lived experiences are not sufficiently honored by civic institutions. Watts and Flanagan ask, "Are young members of marginalized groups as likely as more socially integrated youth to replicate or buy into a system where they feel excluded?" (p. 781).

Just as the content framework for civic education largely fails to embrace the perspectives of all young people, so too does the approach to teaching and learning. Most civic education in U.S. secondary schools today remains stubbornly focused on the procedural elements of democratic society. Noted multicultural education scholar, James Banks (2017), has critiqued the civic learning that many students in experience in schools as a collection of isolated facts about structures, policies, and historical events that are not put in the context of their own identities or experiences in public life, let alone current sociopolitical tensions. Data used to gauge adolescent civic learning and engagement and to construct narratives of youth ignorance or apathy are largely based upon measures of knowledge recall such as multiple choice responses on standardized exams and narrow measures of behavior such as voting (Youniss, 2011). NAEP (2014) acknowledges openly that while young people experience civic education from many sources, including "families, religious institutions, [and] mass media," (p. ix), school-based civic education is strictly "a test of knowledge of skills" (p. vi) of American government and civil society.

This model runs counter to what cutting-edge interdisciplinary science (as represented in recent edited volumes from Nasir et al., 2021 and Lee et al., 2020) tells us about both how learning happens in general and how political socialization occurs in particular. The newest learning science demonstrates that sociopolitical learning is not a narrowly cognitive task but rather a collection of situated practices that occur within overlapping cultural and historical contexts, inextricably linked with identity development and its accompanying affective dimensions. The learning that young people experience during adolescence as they develop a relationship to civic society involves relationships and encounters influenced by considerations of fairness and power, experiences that Bartels (2018) argues most school-based civic education fails to leverage.

Civic instruction that focuses on policies and procedures in the abstract is not designed to support the difficult conversations raised by today's context of structural inequity across multiple aspects of democratic and economic life. This approach participates in the project of seeking to replicate existing civic institutions with incremental improvements. When inequities in civic learning are addressed, they are usually presented as race and class-based opportunity gaps in access to what reports like *Guardians of Democracy: The Civic Mission of Schools* (Gould, 2011) call "best practices'" that uphold this framework. Even when discussions of real-world controversial issues are incorporated into classroom learning, as advocated by civic education scholars, Hess and McAvoy (2016), the focus often narrows to information sources, assigned positions, and pro/con binaries instead of delving into thorny social dynamics. Furthermore, Cohen and colleagues (2012) have critiqued the field of civic education for its struggle to recognize the creative ways that young people are leveraging a variety of multimodal media platforms to express political sentiments and agitate for change.

The contested nature of the civic sphere for all youth, but particularly for youth from historically marginalized communities, raises questions for us about the traditional purposes and practices of civic education. We feel compelled to ask: What does it mean to educate toward civic engagement in a society in which progress does not occur inevitably or in a straight line but instead in stops, starts, and retreats? Whose perspectives and cultural values define progress today? What storylines can inspire civic action when the narrative of the Dream does not resonate? A new wave of civics research and practice is emerging that seeks to shift the center of gravity from integrating young people into current institutions to leveraging the experiences of youth (and the dissonance they often feel) as a catalyst for social dreaming and transformation. Our model of world-building civic education is informed by and extends this wave toward a radically different paradigm for democratic learning.

New Civic Pathways of Action and Imagination

The National Academy of Education (NAEd) recently released a report synthesizing interdisciplinary strands of research related to youth civic reasoning and discourse in order to recommend reformed approaches to civic learning that better integrate student identity and support inquiry-based instruction across secondary school subject areas (Lee et al., 2021). These recommendations emerge amid a shift in civics scholarship as exemplified in the work of Cohen and colleagues (2018) that takes a bottom-up rather than a top-down approach, leveraging students' everyday realities as the catalyst for understanding democratic norms and institutions rather than abstract principles.

This paradigm shift from institutions to students and from characteristics to challenges of democracy can elicit instructional approaches to civic learning that value youth culture, encourage deliberative dialogue, and support local action. Expanding our understanding of public life to consider how youth socialize, organize around issues they care about, and produce complex media across multimodal communication platforms demonstrates how civic engagement can be fundamentally reconceptualized to better fit a culture that is much more participatory than ever before.

As Henry Jenkins and colleagues (2009) explained, "Participatory culture is emerging as the culture absorbs and responds to the explosion of new media technologies that make it possible for average consumers to archive, annotate, appropriate, and recirculate media content in powerful new ways" (p. 8). Although remix culture and fan fiction are seen as some of the main aspects of how participatory culture shapes youth experiences (Jenkins et al., 2015), this includes an important civic shift for youth as well. If youth today possess the tools for producing, distributing, and coordinating civic messages via digital technologies, the opportunities for learning about civic engagement are no longer tethered to traditional spaces like classrooms.

Further, expanding on the value of understanding participatory culture, a group of researchers led by Mimi Ito (2013) have described the ecosystem of extracurricular participation that youth engage in as connected learning. According to Ito and colleagues, connected learning is realized when a young person pursues a personal interest or passion with the support of friends and caring adults and is in turn able to link this learning and interest to academic achievement, career possibilities, or civic engagement (p. 6). By looking at how individuals might collaborate when socializing in virtual worlds like World of Warcraft (Chen, 2011; Nardi, 2010) or Second Life (Boellstorff, 2008;) or online knitting communities (Pfister, 2014) or video game design (Rafalow & Tekinbas, 2014) or fan fiction production (Hellekson & Busse, 2014), connected learning points to powerful forms of participation, engagement, and production that while academically robust is often far removed from school curricula and traditional measures of civic participation.

At the same time, as connected learning points to forms of extracurricular participation that are "socially embedded, interest-driven, and oriented toward educational, economic, or political opportunity" (Ito et al., 2013, p. 6), engagement in online gaming, fan fiction production, and distributing remixes of popular songs can potentially highlight how youth understand their role in broader civic spheres. Youths' lives are spent socializing in digital spaces just as much as they are in their physical environments, and the connected ecosystem must consider how civic learning opportunities occur across these spaces.

Alongside our field's need to challenge what counts as participation, we must consider what kinds of pedagogical approaches ground how we work alongside and within youth-driven civic communities both inside and outside the classroom. While much civic education research treats young people as citizens in training and attempts to measure future commitments to participation in public life rather than honoring their current forms of public engagement, the expanded view of participation that we have presented insists upon highlighting youth civic agency in its own right and on its own terms.

A variety of educational practices in formal and informal educational spaces, running the gamut from ethnic studies courses (Cuauhtin et al., 2019) to hip-hop literacy and culture classes (Kelly, 2020) to youth organizing collaboratives (Kirshner, 2015), are seeking to reorient civic learning from the perspective of young people and build opportunities for action out of the contexts and experiences of their daily lives.

We propose that these practices can be usefully grouped together and understood as forms of civic education under the umbrella of what has come to be known as youth participatory action research (YPAR), a form of inquiry that situates young people as the primary drivers of the research process and situates the issues about which they care most as the primary subjects of that research (Cammarota & Fine, 2008; Duncan-Andrade & Morrell, 2008). While the word research implies that YPAR is primarily a methodology, its openness in terms of the practices that can be included in this term show that its overriding contribution is primarily an epistemological one challenging traditional notions of who can produce knowledge and who can drive social action and change (as we have explored in Mirra, Garcia, & Morrell, 2015).

YPAR happens in a variety of learning contexts, from classrooms and after-school programs to community organizations and universities. It amplifies the voices of young people from elementary school to college and beyond through a range of activities. Our purpose with this quick scan of the field is not to parse exactly which activities should be considered YPAR according to any strict definition, but instead to use YPAR as a broad framework that expands the nature and purpose of civic participation. YPAR addresses key concerns about what counts as research, who gets a voice within the research arena, and what role research plays in the daily lives of youth.

We highlight here a set of competencies distilled from our selected review of YPAR scholarship that comprise a cycle of critical civic learning and development (see Figure 2.1). While these competencies are

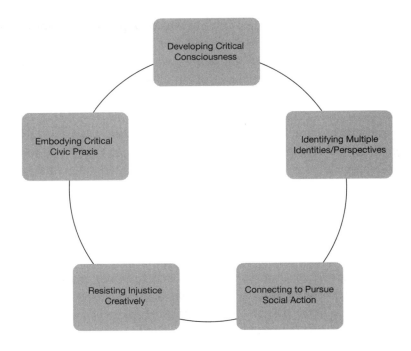

Figure 2.1 Cycle of Critical Civic Learning and Development

inextricably linked in practice, we tease them apart here in order to foreground their unique contributions to challenging traditional models of civic learning and supporting youth agency.

As we unpack each of these competencies, we reiterate they comprise a process that can be used to interrogate the civic world youth and adults inhabit; there is no beginning or end nor linear progression of steps to be followed.

Developing Critical Consciousness

One of the key processes involved in YPAR is the deconstruction of traditional narratives of meritocracy and equality that undergird American Dream mythology and foster deficit ideology about minoritized communities. Unlike most civic education research, YPAR is built upon a critical theoretical tradition, specifically Paulo Freire's

(1970) theory of conscientization, in which oppressed communities engage in critical social analysis in order to expose and dismantle unjust power hierarchies and ideologies and imagine alternative possibilities. Instead of taking at face value the idea that cultural capital is concentrated within dominant communities (Bourdieu, 1985), YPAR draws upon theories that highlight the funds of knowledge (Moll et al., 1992) and cultural wealth (Yosso, 2005) of working-class communities of color.

When describing their influential work with Latinx youth in Tucson, Arizona, Julio Cammarota and Augustine Romero (2011) explain that the development of critical consciousness helps youth move past feelings of powerlessness in the face of civic inequities by helping them "name the practices that counter and address the oppressive social and economic forces impeding the development of a healthy identity, neighborhood, and world" (p. 494). Watts and colleagues (2011) assert that coming to understand society from a critical perspective is the foundation upon which political efficacy and civic praxis can be built.

Identifying Multiple Identities or Perspectives

Part of the process of developing critical consciousness involves making explicit the pluralism of American society, the variety of cultures, experiences, and beliefs that are contained within the label of American citizen. Sonia Nieto and Patty Bode (2008) define multicultural education as the explicit application of critical consciousness to formal and informal learning contexts, transforming not only curriculum and instruction to include diverse perspectives, but also "the interactions among students, teachers, and families and the very way that schools conceptualize the nature of teaching and learning" (p. 44). Critical multicultural education, with its explicit antiracist orientation and commitment to honoring students' lived experiences, sets the stage for characterizing young people as active civic agents with the power to challenge historical power hierarchies and create knowledge on their own terms.

Jason Irizarry (2009) characterizes YPAR as a vehicle for connecting multicultural education to social action in order to counter civic inequities. He highlights youth research as a model that can help young people develop "the skills necessary to positively shape their life trajectories, while simultaneously challenging the multiple forms of oppression that delimit them and reproduce social inequality" (p. 198). This model of civic learning resists conceptualizing Americans as an undifferentiated group and instead celebrates differentiated experience as a catalyst for recognizing oppression and pursuing justice.

Connecting to Pursue Social Action

A key element bridging critical social analysis with social action is a sense of collective efficacy (Watts & Hipolito-Delgado, 2015). YPAR promotes a sense of solidarity and trust between young people and stresses the key role that relationships play in struggles for social justice. YPAR, whether it takes place in schools or community organizations, gives young people opportunities to connect with each other as well as to adults, resources, and experiences that enable them to realize their civic potential and take action on issues that matter to them (Ginwright et al., 2006).

Resisting Injustice Creatively

In the face of oppression, young people can choose to respond in a variety of ways. Daniel Solorzano and Dolores Delgado-Bernal (2001) offer a typology for responses, progressing from reactionary behavior through conformity toward resistance, that hinges upon the extent to which young people possess a critique of social oppression and an orientation toward social justice (p. 318). Without an understanding of oppression created by the ongoing development of critical consciousness, students may veer toward taking action within the constraints of existing civic structures, a choice that the authors claim has little chance of fostering social justice. Transformational resistance is only achieved when young people channel their awareness of oppression and passion for justice into pursuing action that is "political, collective, conscious, and motivated by a sense that individual and social change is possible" (p. 320). YPAR represents a model of civic engagement that has the potential to foster transformational resistance (Caraballo et al., 2017).

Embodying Critical Civic Praxis

Shawn Ginwright and Julio Cammarota (2007) bring together all of the elements of this alternative vision of civic learning in their model of critical civic praxis, which they define as "the organizational processes that promote civic engagement among youth and elevate their critical consciousness and capacities for social justice activism" (p. 699). This commitment to continuous collective action and reflection through YPAR offers a pathway forward in our understanding of how to structure civic learning experiences that resonate with the experiences of young people of color.

YPAR engages productively with the ideas of connected learning and participatory politics considering its commitment to building upon shared youth interests and utilizing digital media tools in the service of amplifying youth voice about issues of civic concern. YPAR scholarship often highlights multimodality as a favored strategy among young people for conducting data collection and sharing their research findings (Yang, 2009). More importantly, YPAR also reinforces the idea that the stance we take toward youth civic participation is just as important, if not more so, than the modalities we use; positioning youth as knowledge-makers necessitates a creative and production-centered relationship with digital technologies.

We argue that these advances in the modalities and stances of civic learning also necessitate new language to describe civic action. We now turn to consider whether the terms "participation" and "engagement" are strong enough to capture the intents and purposes of critical civic praxis and offer new terminology to guide future research in this field.

Speculative Civic Literacies: Moving from Engagement to Innovation

We find it problematic to characterize the critical youth production embodied by participatory culture and YPAR as examples of mere civic participation or engagement, largely because those terms signify action circumscribed by and beholden to a larger system that, in the case of our civic context, is too often attached to patriotic and outdated ideologies and behaviors. While we could be content to claim that these forms of civic learning serve to expand what counts as participation, we feel that the power and potential of these practices call for stronger terminology.

Young people who recognize that their lived experiences do not comport to the narrative of the American Dream and who take social action based on critical social analysis are engaged in the crucial work of interrogating the public sphere. They are disrupting dominant ideas and exposing the bedrock inequities behind the assumptions of fairness and equality in American life. They, like Ta-Nehisi Coates (2015), are taking up the difficult task of moving past the brightly rendered version of their country but finding hope and change in the process of agitation.

They do not stop there. They are not content to ask their questions to those in traditional positions of authority; instead, they turn to the communicative possibilities of new media and raise their voices as researchers to engage in civic innovation. They are remixing tools like Twitter and TikTok through hashtag activism and are beginning to develop their own apps and programs. They are asking adults to take up positions as audience members as young people take the mic to profess their expertise. As quickly as new modes of expression are developed, young people are finding ways to manipulate them to broadcast their civic ideas and beliefs.

These youth practices offer huge promise for challenging systemic inequalities in civic life and for challenging deficit narratives of youth of color in the public sphere. They situate struggle as just as powerful a catalyst for civic action as patriotism and expand our conceptualizations of civic agency.

Yet, even as youth raise their voices and advocate for awareness and change, they continue to witness institutional inertia and unrelenting violence. This frustrating cycle of raised and then dashed hopes led us to question the ability of even the new civics approaches, which still demonstrate faith in the ability of existing democratic institutions and incremental change, to effectively prepare young people with the knowledge, skills, and dispositions to tackle the entrenched public challenges that they continue to face. What if entirely new systems are needed to face these challenges?

Our consideration of these questions drove us to develop new conceptual commitments that push beyond even where student-centered civics takes us. In recent work (Mirra & Garcia, 2020), we developed a theory of speculative civic literacies that encourages boundary-pushing and youth-centered creative thinking about how to reimagine public life. Speculative civic literacies strives to put participatory approaches to democratic learning into conversation with the agentic resistance and public dreaming of futurist literary world building (drawing upon Thomas and Stornaiuolo's (2016) concept of restorying). Our framework is grounded in three interrelated design principles that synthesize interdisciplinary scholarship from the fields of education, history, and literary and cultural studies.

First, speculative civic literacies center informal collective affiliations and relations and decenter the state as the driving force of democratic education. This perspective welcomes youth meaning-making about the nature and purpose of civic community within various contexts before introducing how current governmental structures define those values; instead of immediately seeking to integrate students into systems, it first questions the extent to which systems are responsive to youth needs. This approach has roots in the historical efforts of minoritized communities, particularly Black communities, to create alternative and affirmative understandings of citizenship in the face of persistent legal and institutional exclusion by the state (Hartman, 2019).

These alternative understandings, which manifested themselves through innovations such as mutual aid networks, salons, and art collectives (Spires, 2020), highlight the second principle of the speculative civic literacies framework, which advocates an iterative and practice-based approach to democratic learning. Practice-oriented civic learning that focuses on doing citizenship rather than qualifying as a citizen can dislodge democratic education from the collection-of-facts approach and broaden it beyond the discipline of social studies. Literacy is particularly well-suited to take up this mantle considering its focus on expression and communication. The intellectual history of critical literacy is built upon a foundation of utilizing language for the purpose of analyzing and taking action upon oppressive social systems for the purpose of personal and civic freedom (Morrell, 2008). Research in sociocritical literacy practices across formal and informal learning spaces has long offered multiple examples of young people engaging in expansive forms of sociopolitical learning that are not tied to the narrow knowledge base deemed civic education (Gutiérrez, 2008). Innovative scholarship in civics at the secondary level is increasingly taking such the interdisciplinary approach espoused in the NAEd report, from social studies scholars crossing subject area boundaries (Lo, 2019) to scholars in the fields of math (Kokka, 2019), science (Davis & Schaeffer, 2019), and ethnic studies (Kwon & de los Ríos, 2019) discussing the implications of their work for public life.

Finally, the speculative civic literacies framework seeks to engage in joyful social dreaming even amid uncertainty and continued struggle against injustice. Jenkins et al. (2016) stress the need to think beyond existing social and political levers of change and creatively construct radical new visions of public life as an exercise of civic imagination. Speculative fiction, particularly texts that build upon traditions of Afro- and Indigenous futurisms, embodies the idea that storytelling and the creation of narrative worlds represents a powerful form of resistance and agency in the face of continuing systemic inequities (brown, 2017; Dillon, 2012; Otieno Sumba, 2018). The speculative civic literacies framework is inherently aspirational and contingent as it lives in the very contradictions that undergird U.S. civic life.

Building the Worlds to Come

The model of world-building civic education offered in this book represents our effort to translate the theoretical ideas introduced above into a robust approach to teaching and learning that can be integrated into classroom learning across disciplines and grade levels. The outermost concentric circles in Figure 1.1 of Equity & Justice and Youth Agency remind us that the better worlds that education can help bring into being must be guided by values that honor the full humanity of all, embrace living in relation to each other, and respect young people as collaborators in the construction of new futures.

Each of the world-building commitments at the center of the model—Inquiry, Storytelling, Networking, Imagination, and Advocacy—are interpreted in the chapters to come according to these foundational principles. We have structured the chapters to guide you through the process of rethinking each of these practices and developing strategies for integrating them into your curriculum and instruction. The chapters follow a common structure: First, each commitment is defined and discussed in terms of how it fits into the world-building model; second, we interrogate the problems with how each commitment is traditionally taken up in schools; next, we offer vignettes from the learning communities you met in Chapter 1 to give real-world examples of how to innovate these commitments; and finally, we present concrete strategies that can help you get started with applying the commitments to your practice.

We invite you to make these key moves as you consider each commitment:

- **Inquire** about content, culture, and purpose of our instruction
- **Tell stories** at individual, interpersonal, and community levels
- **Network** within the classroom, beyond the school, and toward freedom
- **Imagine** new civic pathways, magic solutions, and visionary futures
- **Advocate** for, with, and upon our worlds

Let's jump in.

Chapter 3

|||||||||||||||||||

Building the Future
Through Civic Inquiry

"We are going to have to learn to think in radical terms.
I use the term radical in its original meaning—getting
down to and understanding the root cause. It means
facing a system that does not lend itself to your needs and
devising means by which you change that system."

—Ella Baker, from the speech
"The Black Woman in the Civil Rights Struggle" (1969)

All movements for justice originate in the question: "Why?" Inquiry is the engine of social change. Activist and organizer Ella Baker understood this truth on a fundamental level. Often dubbed the mother of the U.S. Civil Rights movement, Baker convened a meeting of college students whose questions and concerns inspired them to join the fight for racial justice in the wake of lunch counter sit-ins in Greensboro, North Carolina, in 1960. Through her guidance, this group would develop into the Student Nonviolent Coordinating Committee (SNCC) and organize some of the most iconic efforts of the struggle. These efforts, including 1964's Freedom Summer, were grounded in education; Baker knew the awesome power of teaching a generation of young people to ask the radical question of "why"—the search for answers lights the spark of public action.

If we want to support our students to build the just world of tomorrow, we must encourage them to think radically and ask the big questions in our classes today. Committing to civic learning in our classrooms does not begin with elaborate projects or days of service;

it begins with the careful cultivation of a spirit of critical inquiry in every aspect of teaching and learning. As Ella Baker reminds us, this spirit needs to embrace the tough work that comes when we encourage students to dig below the surface and question the root causes of why society (and schools) reflect the deep inequities they see around them.

This chapter shares strategies for fostering a culture of civic inquiry grounded in the values of equity and justice to guide the reading, writing, listening, and speaking that your students do in your discipline. We first delve into an exploration of why inquiry is the anchor grounding all of the other world-building civic commitments and then present a guide for interrogating and innovating your approach to inquiry in your practice.

Our journey will focus on taking an inquiry lens toward three core elements of classroom practice: Content, Culture, and Purpose as shown in Table 3.1.

Table 3.1 Interrogating and Innovating with Inquiry

INQUIRY LENS	WHAT TO INTERROGATE	TOOLS TO INNOVATE
Content	1. Whose voices are present (and absent) in our curriculum?	Critical Curriculum Inventory
	2. What messages does our content communicate to students about the values we want to cultivate in civic life?	Civic Literacy Skills
Culture	1. How can we develop an open classroom climate that reflects the kind of society in which we want to live?	Cogenerative Civic Dialogues
	2. What routines can we develop alongside students that support them to advocate for what they need in school and beyond?	Restorative/ Reparative Teaching

INQUIRY LENS	WHAT TO INTERROGATE	TOOLS TO INNOVATE
Purpose	1. What world is our teaching striving to bring into being?	World-Building Essential Questions
	2. How can we foreground the civic goals of teaching in our planning and practice?	Community Connections

The Importance of Civic Inquiry: Community and Classroom Contexts

Let's return to Ella Baker's quote for a moment. As she continued this speech, she explained that questioning inequity does not immediately lead to change. She added, "But one of the things that has to be faced is, in the process of wanting to change that system, how much we have got to do to find out *who we are, where we come from,* and *where we are going.*"

Inquiry is crucial to improving civic life because one question about society can lead to many more complex questions about our histories and identities in the communities in which we live, as well as about the operation of institutions in society and our dreams for the future. Seeking answers to these questions together builds solidarity and momentum and leads to more creative and focused problem-solving efforts. We cannot change what we cannot see; good questions serve as lenses to sharpen our view.

We suggest that the rationale for privileging a culture of civic inquiry in the classroom is not only or even primarily about preparing young people for formal acts of democratic engagement like voting. Instead, we are more interested in how a commitment to inquiry can support youth to approach their informal, day-to-day interactions with neighbors from a stance of curiosity and common purpose and come together to advocate for change in multiple forms.

Consider contemporary social movements spearheaded by youth around the world about issues such as gun violence and climate change. These movements were sparked when individual young people asked questions about specific challenges close to home; for example, why did a mass shooting occur in my community? Why are extreme weather events happening so often where I live? These questions are important and often lead to some immediate stopgap measures such as lockdown drills and sea walls.

Yet in the process of joining in dialogue with others from a range of perspectives and life experiences, youth organizers found that more questions began to proliferate, exposing root issues and deepening the problems that needed to be addressed. For example, what role does racial identity play in media coverage and government response to gun violence? Why do communities that experience poverty tend to experience more severe effects related to global warming? Will the earth be safe and habitable when I grow up?

Posing these questions demonstrates the qualities of thoughtfulness, nuance, and civic consciousness that young people will need as they begin tackling the serious local and global challenges their generation will inherit. These questions are the spark of social action. While families and teachers cannot predict the crises our children will face in the decades ahead, we can and must prepare them with an education that enables them to question society and tackle whatever shortcomings they find with a spirit of equity, empathy, and justice.

As discussed in the previous chapter, the principles of youth participatory action research (YPAR) ground us in the belief that the ultimate sign of respect for young people as developing civic leaders involves engaging them in honest and open dialogue about society's challenges and honoring their experiences and perspectives. From kindergarten through college, youth are asking questions about the world around them. They are ready to explore the most challenging issues, and they need us to trust and support them.

INQUIRY IN ACTION: ASKING QUESTIONS LIKE *FOXFIRE*

While inquiry may be seen as the start of larger endeavors in our classrooms, sometimes just asking questions is the first innovative act in and of itself. Articulating an ethos of questioning can be its own civically actionable outcome in our classrooms.

One historical example is the work of educator Eliot Wiggington and the *Foxfire* magazine and, later, books (1968) he cocreated with his students. Working in a Georgia-based secondary school in the 1960s, Wiggington sought to create a venue where local expertise and cultural practices were preserved.

His students began a decades-long project of interviewing community members about various aspects of Appalachian culture. From beading to fishing to moonshining, the *Foxfire* publications preserve and amplify the cultural practices that are not typically encountered in history books or treated respectfully in popular media. Recounting the origins of *Foxfire*, Wiggington recalls wondering why and how people used the stages of the moon to guide their planting and farming practices and asking students to investigate: "They went home and talked—really talked—to their own relatives, some of them for the first time. From those conversations came superstitions, old home remedies, weather signs, a story about a hog hunt, a taped interview with the retired sheriff about the time the local bank was robbed—and directions for planting by the signs" (1968, p. 11).

The first collection of student writing, *The Foxfire Book* (Wiggington, 1968), includes a more than 50-page explanation of how to build a log cabin, followed by the necessary chapter on chimney building, chapters about snake lore, faith healing, soap making, and much, much more. It is playful, exploratory, and rooted in intergenerational exploration of the everyday lives of family and community.

Unlike other projects that we will describe, sharing the narratives that students collected from local community members was Wiggington's culminating outcome. Rather than seeing interviews as data points for larger takeaways and recommendations, these Foxfire stories are about asking questions as a means of preservation and dissemination of local genius: "Daily our grandparents are moving out of our lives, taking with them, irreparably, the kind of information contained in this book," writes Wiggington (1968, p. 12).

Recognizing this as a universal challenge, he calls for students and educators alike to ask questions of those around them. Further, as an activity designed by a teacher and successfully enacted across multiple decades, *Foxfire* is a powerful template of action-based inquiry that can be adapted in multiple classroom settings. Wiggington's work reminds us that the voices of our community are too often overlooked in the media and in our own civic actions. As students encounter disciplinary concepts in our classrooms—whether it be the impacts of colonialism, the symbolism in Shakespearean texts, or the meaning of quantitative data or statistics—these are topics that might encourage us to actively investigate and ask:

- Whose voices and perspectives are left out?
- What might those at the business or community center down the street say in response to the information being shared?
- Whose perspectives could we invite into our classrooms?

This last point, importantly, is not a hypothetical one. With a bit of planning by you or by your students, local civic leaders, business representatives, and organizers can visit your classroom in person or via online software. Further, ensuring that your students are doing so safely, interviewing members of the community can expand the world to which your classroom exposes students. This might mean starting small and asking students to gauge the views and perspectives of a sibling or family member, or doing more robust research on a topic and engaging in systematic outreach to various constituents within a geographic area. Importantly, the only reason we can share the work and innovation of *Foxfire* is because these students published the voices and perspectives they captured in their interviews. With online resources, students might create similar *Foxfire*-inspired anthologies in their own classrooms.

Brazilian educator Paulo Freire (1970) offers a contrast between "banking" and "problem-posing" models of instruction to illustrate what teaching and learning looks like when inquiry is valued (or not valued) in the classroom. The banking model represents the absence of inquiry: the teacher has already decided the content and skills that students should learn about a given subject area topic and proceeds to deposit this information into students' minds for them to absorb and echo on assessments. The problem-posing model, on the other hand, centers inquiry: the teacher designs provocative questions related to relevant and authentic issues in their subject area and invites students to explore those questions collaboratively. Instead of being expected to meet pre-determined outcomes, the teacher and students engage in a journey of academic and civic discovery together to end somewhere new.

The question for us to consider is: Which model is utilized more often in the U.S. education system? In our schools? In our own class-room? Let's dive in.

Interrogating the Traditional Role of Inquiry in Schools

The use of the banking metaphor to describe rote models of teach-ing and learning brings to mind another metaphor for schooling that does not exactly invoke associations with creativity: a factory. The term "factory model school" originates in rhetoric related to the industrial revolution in the early- and mid-20th century; it brings to mind images of identical classrooms in which young people are seated in neat rows dutifully accomplishing identical tasks. The rationale for this model is the ability to educate large numbers of students efficiently in prepara-tion for the repetitive labor waiting for them in the job market. Inquiry and creativity are not necessary or desirable in this model; it would slow down the production line.

Fast forward to today's educational landscape, filled with buzzwords like 21st-century learning and future-ready schools. The effects of eco-nomic globalization and advances in digital communication technolo-gies have pushed those in the field to consider educational approaches that replace concerns with standardization and replicability with a drive toward individualization and originality.

Why then do the images of industrial-era classrooms still look so familiar to us today?

Many schools have taken steps to move toward more inquiry-driven frameworks for instruction, but a wide swath of the public education system still operates in a hierarchical, mechanical fashion more appropriate for churning out widgets than sparking young minds. Disturbingly, but not so surprisingly, the factor that often separates these categories of schools is the race and class composition of the student body. Generations of educational researchers have consistently demonstrated that students of color and students in high-poverty schools are more likely to be denied the progressive pedagogies that their white and affluent peers enjoy (Anyon, 1980; Valenzuela, 1999).

This reality raises questions: Who gets to ask questions about society? Who gets to dream? In your own classroom, what does dreaming look like for your students? How might you expand the possibilities and the scope for dreaming within your content area and in the confined space of your classroom?

In your own classroom, name the contexts for encouraging young people to ask open-ended questions:

- When do these opportunities show up?
- How are they investigated?
- How do you help the quieter students in your class find pathways to asking and exploring besides raising their hands?

Consider the kindergartners you know and you will be reminded that all young people have an amazing ability to ask questions, and they often possess the creativity and compassion to imagine radical solutions to civic challenges. What happens as they grow up? Among many influences, we cannot ignore the influence of school in dampening this spirit.

Even when schools adopt frameworks of inquiry-based learning, curriculum and instruction are often still circumscribed within the bounds of "schooled" thinking. For example, the scope and sequence of units and prescribed content in subject areas and grade levels may stay the same—determined by adults according to their needs—but those unit titles may be replaced by more jazzy names. Students may be offered a level of individual preference in reading material or summative assessment topics, but only insofar as they pick from the menu of choices provided by the teacher. Real-world issues may be voiced in relation to the disciplinary content being discussed, but warily and without related engagement.

These approaches to inquiry can end up amounting to putting a new cover on the same book. Preparing students for the challenges of today and tomorrow requires us to disrupt and ultimately deconstruct the barriers we construct between school and society and take youth seriously as civic leaders.

Innovating Our Commitment to Inquiry: Moving From Theory to Practice

Truly innovating our commitment to inquiry in our work as educators requires us to take leaps forward in our thinking about the practice and purpose of education. We suggest three major shifts that need to take place in how we think about our: (1) content, (2) culture, and (3) purpose.

In this section, we offer vignettes from three of the meaningful learning communities we have codesigned with teachers and youth. After each story, we break down how the practices described can serve as inspiration for redesigning your approach to inquiry in your own practice. This journey may seem daunting, but small moves lead to radical acts. Let's explore the concrete steps you can take to get started. Then take your practice to the next level when you're ready.

Inquiring about Content

A policy debate case, like many other genres of writing practiced in the literacy classroom, follows a prescriptive set of norms. In debate, the format is similar to an argumentative essay, except that instead of thesis statements, students who participate in U.S. youth debate tournaments offer hypothetical policy proposals that they believe the federal government should adopt about whatever the league's yearly resolution is. They then offer claims, evidence, and warrants to support their case and develop counterarguments against the opposing team in the hopes of convincing a judge to declare them the winners of a round. Students have to prepare two cases (pro and con) and be prepared to argue both as they move from round to round.

The student debaters at Middle School 50 in Brooklyn, New York, were becoming pretty successful at following this format. Their teacher, Mr. Warren, taught them the formula—policy, claim, evidence, warrant—and drilled them on switching positions on an issue. Yet something shifted during the 2019–2020 school year when they learned the resolution they would be debating: "Resolved: The U. S.'s federal government should substantially reduce its restrictions on legal immigration to the United States."

The team faced a dilemma: Were they supposed to just follow the format and debate against and for immigration restrictions as if the topic had no personal resonance with them? Almost all of them were either immigrants or the children of immigrants. This was about their families, their community. How could they just follow the script?

Instead of directing them to simply follow the rules of this academic exercise, Mr. Warren reflected upon the nature of the activity itself. Is debating both sides of every issue always an ethical choice when the rhetoric on one side of the immigration issue so often involves questioning the humanity of a group of people? How could he support his students to stand up for what they believed in while still participating in tournaments?

After much deliberation, Mr. Warren and the team forged a new path. They would develop one case that they would use in their rounds whether they were assigned to be pro or con. The case would question the traditional norms of debate and of U.S. policy about immigration and ask their opponents and judges to join them in a new inquiry: What if we imagined a borderless society instead?

The story of the Middle School 50 debate team (which will continue in the chapters to come) serves as a reminder that the practices in our discipline—the content that we read, the genres in which we write—are never neutral. The academic literacy exercises that we assign to our students implicitly reflect values about desirable forms of communication in our society. Whose voices or perspectives are present and absent in our curriculum? What messages do our writing assignments send about how we expect young people to dialogue with each other in public?

Taking an inquiry stance on our curriculum requires us to interrogate the values that undergird what we teach and to then innovate our practice by breaking away from familiar outlines and formats. It requires us to adopt a spirit of experimentation guided by commitments to equity and agency and make the conscious decision to connect academic content and skills to their application in civic life.

Getting Started: Critical Curriculum Inventory. The pace of the school year does not readily lend itself to reflection; the next period's students are always on their way in the door and the next day's lessons need to be planned. Nonetheless, we can take a small step toward adopting a commitment to inquiry in our content by reserving some time to review our curricular materials for the semester or year and engaging in a critical curriculum inventory.

Such an inventory (see Table 3.2) involves noticing the voices, topics, knowledge, and skills that are present explicitly and implicitly in what we teach, critically analyzing the assumptions and embedded messages that these presences and absences send students about literacy in public life, and taking steps to align purpose to practice. This inquiry activity can be startling and even painful as it reveals the ingrained biases that often accumulate within school curriculum over years and become the received common sense of teaching. Accept this discomfort as the first step toward clarifying commitments and changing practice.

If you find that your content largely privileges the voices of individuals whose identities in the areas of race, gender, religion, sexual orientation, country of origin, and other social categories reflect historically inequitable power structures, ask yourself: Is this the range of voices that students encounter in society? World-building civics instruction is committed to analyzing and then transforming the world in which

Table 3.2   Content Inventory

CONTENT INVENTORY INQUIRY QUESTIONS	WHAT TO INTERROGATE	HOW TO INNOVATE
Whose voices are represented?	Identity categories of the authors and characters in course texts	Diversify text selection
Which topics are explored?	Themes and experiences explored in course texts	Make intentional choices to explore topics that resonate with students' civic interests and experiences
What knowledge is deemed valuable?	Information that students are required to comprehend about particular disciplines	Broaden perceptions of knowledge and orient information toward the purpose of equity and agency in public life
What skills are practiced?	Literacy skills that students are required to master	Expand the range of skills that demonstrate students' literacies and focus on the skills needed for civic participation

we live today in all of its beauty, struggle, and controversy; this provides a mandate for diversifying the curriculum in terms of the voices welcomed into the room and the topics addressed. The #DisruptTexts movement (Ebarvia, 2020) is a powerful catalyst for inquiry and ideas for reimagining what we teach and why.

Similarly, if you find that the knowledge and skills that students are exposed to in your class are narrowly focused on academic outcomes such as standardized exams (e.g., preparing for the formulaic argumentative essay), ask yourself: Does this capture the range of literacies that students encounter in society? Being able to critically analyze the discourse moves in TikTok videos can be just as consequential for navigating civic life as analyzing figurative language in a canonical novel. If not more consequential. Instead of relying on the idea of transfer and assuming that students can just apply subject area skills to the real world once they leave our class, we must remember that our class is part of the real world. Thus, it should engage with the multiple literacies that proliferate in our students' lives right now.

Taking It to the Next Level: Civic Literacy Skills. Once we have completed this inventory and committed to making changes in our practice, we can begin the deeper work of ensuring that the skills we address in each of our units are purposefully conceptualized as civic literacy skills. This means that we do not simply teach students how language works; we teach students how language works to accomplish particular aims in civic and political life and how they in turn can harness those tools to advocate for themselves and their communities.

For example, instead of requiring students to simply learn the difference between similes and metaphors in isolation, we can make the shift to teaching them about the power of figurative language to shape public messaging about controversial civic issues. This small shift puts skills in the service of a deeper purpose, injecting relevance into the curriculum and opening the doors to authentic writing assessments that can live in the world beyond your bag of papers to grade. Instead of a traditional literary analysis essay, perhaps students investigate the elements of a piece of protest art.

Each of the units you plan is likely structured around a particular subset of standards (e.g., Common Core). When you are ready to make bigger changes to these units, write out each of the standards and think about how the skills embedded in them are used in the context of civic engagement (see Table 3.3). These are your civic literacy skills. You can build upon these to transform your summative assessments. Perhaps you change a writing assignment to address a real-world topic or have students write an argument about a community challenge that they actually present to local officials.

Table 3.3   Civic Literacy Skills

STANDARD	CIVIC LITERACY SKILLS	POTENTIAL SUMMATIVE ASSESSMENTS

Inquiring about Culture

The students and teachers of the Council of Youth Research (CYR), an extracurricular YPAR community in Los Angeles, California, could not ignore the looming anniversary of the Williams v. California decision. The California Supreme Court had determined way back in 2004 that all students in the state were entitled to a quality education and that public schools needed to be held accountable for providing equal access to that education. As another school year began, however, the youth researchers looked around at their still-underfunded classrooms and asked: What kind of education do we truly deserve, and how do we get what we are entitled to?

The CYR group from Manual Arts High School decided to focus on defining "quality" curriculum. They researched how young people learned best and reflected upon the most powerful learning experiences in their own lives. They read about critical and culturally relevant approaches to education. The common threads that they found were that students needed to see their lives and interests reflected in class activities and that they needed to be treated as partners in the learning process.

These findings led them to further questions; for instance, if models exist for more engaging curriculum and instruction, how could they encourage teachers to adopt these models and change their practice? Instead of continuing to focus only on how young people learn, they began to also think about how adults learn. They determined that teachers also needed hands-on experiences with new concepts. During one team meeting, 11th-grader Patricia suggested, "What if we run a meeting to teach the teachers what we need?"

Some of the students were a bit intimidated. Would teachers be willing to learn from their students? Everyone was so used to things being the other way around. How would it feel for young people to run a professional development session for adults and ask for the quality education they needed? They decided to find out.

This story reminds us that commitments to inquiry involve not only interrogating our disciplinary content but also our relationships to our students and the classroom culture that we cultivate with them. The intimidation that the CYR students from Manual Arts High School felt at the idea of teaching their teachers reflects the continued prevalence of hierarchical thinking and lopsided conceptions of power in schools. We have been socialized to believe that teachers do the teaching and students do the learning; teachers exert power and students submit to it. Yet supporting students as developing civic leaders demands that we deconstruct these beliefs and create new norms of collaboration.

Freire (1970) believed that the ideal learning environment involved fluid and horizontal (rather than top-down) relationships in which all participants were both teacher–students and student–teachers. Prompting students to ask questions of the texts they read but to unquestioningly acquiesce to the participation structures that their teachers put in place sends contradictory messages that stymie student agency. How can we develop an open classroom climate that reflects the kind of society in which we want to live? What routines can we develop with our students to ensure that they have the opportunity and invitation to advocate for what they need from us as their teachers?

Getting Started: Cogenerative Civic Dialogues. Children and teenagers are very attuned to questions of fairness. They are experts at calling out hypocrisy when they see it. We've all heard the expression,

"Do as I say, not as I do"—and we all know how frustrating it is when those we trust do not practice what they preach. Unfortunately, schools have historically been contradictory and hypocritical spaces when it comes to preparing youth to become civic leaders; while students are encouraged to raise their voices and advocate for what they need in society, they are often told to lower those voices and do what they are told in the classroom. If we truly believe that young people are not just the citizens of tomorrow but citizens today, what message does it send if we do not engage them as partners in designing the routines and structures of our classrooms and schools?

While formal efforts like student governance councils are important in this regard, informal practices in our classrooms are just as crucial to respecting the civic autonomy and agency of our students. For example, science and hip-hop educator Christopher Emdin (2016), instituted cogenerative dialogues, what he calls "cogens," in his classroom with the goal of "cocreating/generating plans of action for improving the classroom" (p. 65). He invited small, revolving groups of students to meet with him over lunch or after school in order to learn more about what was or wasn't working in terms of how he organized learning in the classroom and collaborated with them to try new approaches.

At first glance, cogens may seem simple, as if we are just asking for student feedback for the purposes of improvement as we hopefully always do. What makes cogens much more complex and civically powerful in the classroom is the intentional effort to situate students as valued codesigners in the learning process whose knowledge about their pedagogical needs is fundamental to the functioning of the learning environment. When we as teachers open up space to welcome inquiry about our instructional practices in a spirit of vulnerability and true partnership with youth, we disrupt the hierarchies of education and society and model critical civic dialogue.

Taking It to the Next Level: Restorative Teaching. Don't be discouraged if you find during your first few attempts at cogens that students are experiencing difficulty articulating what they need from you as their teacher or how they might like to reorganize the routines of the classroom. Sadly, this difficulty is to be expected in a system that has often socialized young people to believe that they do not have the knowledge or the right to have a say in the form and purpose of their own education.

Cogens represent one small step in the larger project of resocializing ourselves and our students into a mindset where we can define what humanizing civic education should be. There are so many relationships within schools that need to be restored to take on less of a consumer mentality and more of a civic mentality: the relationships between administrators and teachers, teachers and students, and all school representatives with families and community members. Use the practice of cogens as a springboard to consider how the restoration of relationships guided by values of equity and agency can contribute to more extensive partnerships and collaborative dreaming about the society we want to create for our young people.

Inquiring about Purpose

The six high school English teachers participating in the Digital Democratic Dialogue (3D) Project logged on to the monthly team Zoom meeting from their various locations around the United States. It was four months into the school year and the students in each of their classes had already chosen civic issues they wanted to discuss with their peers and been organized into cross-school online discussion groups that students could access during the school day. The teachers had been working long hours to figure out how to integrate this innovative project into the existing curricular requirements of their courses and this was their chance to check in with each other.

"My students are so excited. They said that they had never talked to anyone from Alaska before!" Peter said. Voices overlapped as the teachers shared how much their students were enjoying the chance to talk to students from communities that often differed significantly from their own. The students were discussing complex civic issues—climate change, criminal justice, racial inequity—and sharing the experiences from their own lives that contributed to their developing views about them.

"This turned out to be such an amazing extension of the unit

I usually teach about persuasive speeches," Molly said. "We talk about what it means to raise your voice about what matters to you and to do so in a way that invites others to connect with you. Now they are practicing it in real time!" The teachers recounted stories of students whose perspectives on controversial issues were being expanded by hearing the stories of others.

The teachers had joined this 3D Project learning community because they wanted to learn more about how they could incorporate civic learning into their English Language Arts (ELA) curriculum. Now, watching their students engaging in authentic civic dialogue, they wondered how this could change their entire approach to teaching literacy. Janelle asked, "Isn't my job to help students learn how to have tough conversations with a spirit of empathy so that they can change the world?"

This story exemplifies what can happen when we apply commitments to inquiry to our subject area content and to our relationships with students and colleagues. We gain the confidence and creativity to begin asking the deeper questions about why we do what we do and what the purpose of education should be in a democratic society. By taking a leap into a professional learning community that supported them to experiment with new practices, the teachers of the 3D Project were able to reconnect with goals for their teaching that extended far beyond academic skill development. Teaching literacy became about laying the groundwork for a more compassionate public sphere.

Once we come to understand and experience the critical civic importance of education, we can begin the lifelong professional journey of designing all of our practices with intentionality and care to revolve around this goal. Rather than conceptualizing inquiry as one more thing to think about atop all of our other responsibilities as we plan lessons and units, committing to inquiry offers us a lens through which to understand and improve everything we already do with a renewed sense of purpose.

Getting Started: World-Building Essential Questions.   When you think of the projects and units and ideas and dreams that you hope are explored in your classroom, what are the orienting questions that you want your students to encounter? While this chapter encourages you to make room for your students to ask big questions and to passionately hunt down fulfilling answers to these questions, you should begin naming the questions that will guide your classroom activities. We are calling these questions—the ones that might orient your units for unlocking powerful civic promise in you and your students—*world-building essential questions*. These are often big questions. In coauthor Nicole's classroom, she organized student learning around a question that still drives much of our work as researchers and teacher educators today: How can we use our literacy skills to fight for justice in an unjust world?

In a year-long project-based learning curriculum that coauthor Antero codesigned for 9th-grade students (Boardman et al., 2021), student learning opportunities were organized around the questions: "How is the world composed for us? And how do we compose our world?" These democratic essential questions should be provocative and open-ended enough for multiple lines of inquiry. Rich exploration for students and creative lesson design for teachers can both flourish productively and synergistically. While you might have hunches about how to begin answering these essential questions, we encourage you to design these so that you are simultaneously exploring these questions for yourself alongside your students.

Depending on your teaching context, you might feel constrained when thinking of your essential questions. The pacing guides in your department, the required texts and content, a calendar year that feels relentless in disrupting your fluid lesson plans: these are all legitimate challenges we know many of you face. By beginning with timeless and intriguing questions, you can often use these limitations as sources for inquiry and begin to mold the required and fixed elements of your teaching into powerful learning opportunities and spaces for critique.

Taking It to the Next Level: Community Connections. Now that you've got an essential question, it is time to take those questions beyond your classroom and beyond the school walls into community spaces. Consider the physical and social networks you have: What are intriguing groups and individuals that can help spark learning in your classroom? Are there local organizations that are aligned with your questions? Provocateurs who will help challenge student thinking? Intergenerational experts, including students' family members, who can shed light on the nuances of local contexts related to these questions? When coauthor Antero was teaching in Los Angeles, he was able to partner with a middle school teacher and they ended up collaborating with representatives from the City of Los Angeles around understanding local contexts of graffiti and muraling. Likewise, when thinking about environmental challenges in the dense metropolis, he recruited a group called the Guerilla Gardeners to offer a hands-on exploration of how to transform local areas through gardening public spaces. These guests and partnerships expand the possibilities of your classroom.

While it may be daunting to reach out to strangers in this way, the rewards and long-term partnerships are often worth it. In our experiences, government representatives, nonprofit organizations, and local artists and activists often welcome the opportunity to interact with and support young people. While you may get a "no" from busy people, that is an easy answer to receive; move on to inviting someone else to help enliven your classroom learning. As you begin building out transformative lesson plans, start brainstorming people you can recruit. Better yet, consider embedding this research-and-reach-out activity as something to do with your students rather than for them.

Why Not?

"Some people see things as they are and say, 'why'?
I dream things that never were and say, 'why not?'"
—Robert F. Kennedy (1968)
(paraphrasing George Bernard Shaw)

It takes a tremendous amount of trust and vulnerability to open up your classroom to the unknowing and powerful echo of "why." When we create opportunities for student questioning, we open up the worlds of our classrooms to the legacies of civic possibilities that leaders like Ella Baker and Robert F. Kennedy—whose voices bookend this chapter—spoke of. In shaping the content, the culture, and the purposes of our classrooms, a commitment to inquiry acts as the bedrock upon which transformative learning builds continuously, purposefully, and collectively.

Importantly, while much of this chapter rightly centers the inquiry of young people in our classrooms, we also recognize your brilliance as educators and the myriad questions we may hold at bay on any given day in our classrooms. We encourage educators to take a parallel stance to students who are asking hard questions. The open classroom climate and the habits and routines that mediate powerful learning for young people also allow your own questions to trickle into action and collective imagination with colleagues and partners within your school and beyond. Building on the work of Marilyn Cochran-Smith and Susan Lytle (2009), we encourage teachers to take on inquiry as a "stance": "a grounded theory of action that positions the role of practitioners and practitioner knowledge as central to the goal of transforming teaching, learning, leading, and schooling" (p. 119).

Asking questions as teachers and as a collective of inquirers with our young people requires us to find the means to unravel the injustices that are endemic in our classrooms and society today. As our reparative model of teaching suggests, this is work that encourages you to move beyond fixed notions of schooling and the systems of content delivery designed within them. Rather, by moving to an ethos of "why not?" we are building a new world of possibilities.

Discussion Questions

As you read this chapter and work through possibilities for your classroom context, we encourage you to discuss the following questions with your colleagues:

1. Looking at the commitments to inquiry that open this chapter, how would you describe the content, culture, and purpose of your classroom? Who defines these and how do students shape them?
2. This chapter starts from the premise that civic movements are built on the premise of asking why and how injustices persist. What

issues or topics drive you personally and professionally? What questions are at the heart of these topics today and historically?

3. When you think of democratizing your classroom culture and promoting an openness with inquiry, what are the biggest barriers you face? What will you do to address these?

4. Social transformation and better pedagogy don't start with the small: What are the big questions you have as a teacher and for your classroom content? How can you strive to shape your teaching career and your classroom practice to address these topics?

Chapter 4

Building the Future Through Civic Storytelling

To build upon the previous chapter's focus on the civic power of inquiry, we offer another question: Once our students begin inquiring into the world around them, how can we structure learning opportunities in our disciplines to support their curiosity and foster their agency?

If you are anything like us, your instincts might initially point you toward activities that have long been considered best practices of civic learning: debates about current events, political simulations like town halls, or research papers and presentations. Several common threads link these activities—the privileging of informational texts, the foregrounding of analytical thinking, and the centering of formal civic institutions.

These activities and skills of course have a valuable role to play in our classrooms, but upon further reflection, we wonder about the opportunities for world building that we withhold from our students if we interpret civic education too narrowly. Will young people be prepared to tackle novel social challenges if the social and political horizons we offer them are so tightly tethered to existing facts, policies, and institutions? Understanding familiar norms can only take us all so far in the journey toward a more equitable society. What youth crave are new narratives of connection and possibility.

In this chapter, we propose that individual and collective storytelling is just as important—if not more important—to civic education as analysis and argumentation. We offer strategies for integrating stories into inquiry-centered civic learning across subject areas. We begin by delving into the crucial role that narratives play in understanding ourselves and society, particularly in today's polarized political context. We then interrogate the civic messages embedded in the communication structures that we tend to valorize in school. Finally, we offer innovative classroom tools and examples demonstrating that when we encourage our students to answer questions with stories before arguments, we create the conditions within which dialogue, empathy, and common civic purpose can take root.

Our exploration will highlight three interrelated narrative forms we can cultivate in our practice: individual, interpersonal, and community stories (see Table 4.1).

Table 4.1   Interrogating and Innovating with Storytelling

STORYTELLING LENS	WHAT TO INTERROGATE	TOOLS TO INNOVATE
Individual	1. How do our students' personal stories intersect with our class content and civic life? 2. To what extent do we take up our students' stories in the design and delivery of our instruction?	Autoethnography Disrupting Disciplinary Norms
Interpersonal	1. How can we support students to engage with the stories of others from a starting point of understanding rather than argument?	Stance/Value Dialogues Inter-Community Dialogues
Community	1. What lessons can we apply from the experience of storytelling to develop a more humanizing democratic community?	Recognizing Media Tropes Community Counternarratives

The Importance of Civic Storytelling:
Classroom and Community Contexts

"We tell ourselves stories in order to live."

—Joan Didion (2006)

Didion's quote is not merely a metaphor. Stories play a fundamental role in what it means to be human in multiple ways. First, we construct our identities through stories. Think about how you respond to the common getting-to-know-you prompt, "Tell me about yourself." We automatically launch into narrative, choosing which relationships, characteristics, and interests to highlight or downplay as we seek to define ourselves. Studies of the brain have demonstrated that the structure of stories captures our attention and can be processed more easily than other forms of information amid our consistent media overload (Mar & Oatley, 2008; Zadbood et al., 2017).

Crucially, these stories of ourselves are inherently social. Each element of our individual identities is tied up in various communities: those we choose to identify with, those with whom others identify us, and those we forge together or impose upon each other. Storytelling is the glue that binds us. The nature of the stories we tell simultaneously reflects and brings into being the society we create. The concentric circles of community that ripple out from and surround a single person— family, friends, neighborhoods, schools, all the way up through nations and global sociopolitical orders—derive their power and standing from the stories we tell and the stories we believe.

It can be difficult to think about the physical institutions or social principles that structure our lives in terms of story. Their materiality can become so ingrained in what is considered common sense that we forget humans just like us decided to tell a story and over time it gained enough legitimacy to become taken for granted as a given. Sometimes we only come to see the power stories have over the conditions of our lives when those taken-for-granted tales are interrupted or remixed to reveal something new.

Take for example the impact of the 1619 Project. The brainchild of journalist Nikole Hannah-Jones, it began as a special edition of the

New York Times Magazine in 2019 and has subsequently grown into a multimedia collection of essays, films, art, and curricular resources (published in 2021) all dedicated to asking the provocative question: What if we shifted our understanding of the founding of the United States from the year 1776 to the year 1619, when the first ship carrying enslaved people from Africa arrived in what is now Virginia? This narrative shift to name slavery rather than freedom as the original bedrock of this country's democracy casts many public institutions in a new light. From housing to the criminal justice system, from history textbooks to voting rights, the project encouraged citizens to consider today's social inequities as rooted in structural decisions rather than individual pathologies.

The intense media attention and political firestorm that the 1619 Project generated is a testament to both the central role that stories play in structuring our views of the world around us and the power of storytelling to catalyze social change. Those who object to the Project's narrative have not simply expressed their concerns; they have frequently sought to ban the teaching of its content in schools. To literally fear the prospect of young people encountering perspectives about their country that diverge from a mainstream narrative shows that narratives uphold an existing social status quo—and can disrupt it. As Hannah-Jones (2021) herself has noted, "The fights over the 1619 project, like most fights over history, at their essence are about power" (p. xviii).

Indeed, the drive to maintain and protect the integrity of the stories that undergird our civic and political ideologies and material reality can lead to us rejecting information that threatens those narrative structures. Joseph Kahne and Benjamin Bowyer (2017) have written about the challenges posed to civic education by the proliferation of politically motivated misinformation in these polarized times when individuals often decline to believe factual information about civic and political issues that do not conform to their tightly held ideologies. These findings suggest that placing trust in fact-checking and evidence-based argumentation to promote understanding and common cause between citizens is insufficient; social change requires not only shifts in the information we consume but also in the stories we share.

It is unsurprising that schools are the prime target for battles over civic storytelling, considering the influential role they play in socializing us into particular narratives about constructs such as race, gender, and national identity. Critical race theorists in the field of education have long grappled with how the stories we learn in school perpetuate social inequities. Tara Yosso (2005a) defines majoritarian stories as those that "recount the experiences and perspectives of those with racial and social privilege" (p. 9). These stories can be about communities, such as those that label students from minoritized communities as "at-risk" or characterize their families as uninvolved. The stories can also be about curricular content, influencing which historical figures emerge as heroes or which authors deserve to have their novels taught as canon. When paired with the power to control school structures such as funding, resources, and discipline, these stories calcify privilege and oppression.

Yosso (2005a) situates counter-storytelling as an integral element of dismantling these oppressive systems. Counter-stories include the testimony of individuals sharing personal perspectives and experiences that disrupt majoritarian narratives; they also include a wide range of popular culture and art that seek to decenter social norms such as whiteness and heteronormativity and tell new stories that seed the potential for alternative social futures. Movies like *Black Panther* that inject Afrofuturist perspectives into the superhero genre demonstrate how tools of mass communication that have been and continue to be employed to perpetuate mainstream narratives can also be leveraged to tell different stories. Even if youth do not see stories that reflect varied experiences, they are increasingly creating new narratives themselves. Ebony Elizabeth Thomas and Amy Stornaiuolo (2016) discuss how young people who do not see themselves portrayed in the media are "restorying" public life through digital media practices such as fan fiction and remixing to "create their own textual representations and push back against dominant portrayals" (p. 316).

Counter-storytelling can be more powerful than information in opening people's minds and hearts to different perspectives. While facts can cause individuals to dig into their entrenched beliefs, personal stories can alter individuals' political sympathies by offering a window into our common humanity. Generations of artists and educators have praised the power of storytelling to help young people step outside of their own experiences and empathize with others. Yet what critical race theorists remind us is that empathy is not something that can be conceptualized only at the individual level; instead, it is a habit of mind that must be cultivated with explicit attention to power, privilege, and the social constructs that differentiate our experiences. In coauthor Nicole's previous work (2018), she has discussed the need for educators to forge a critical civic perspective on empathy with their students that delves into the thorny politics embedded in the stories that structure our lives and orients storytelling toward equitable social action.

If we want our students to be able to build compassionate futures that embrace an expansive range of experiences and perspectives, we would be well served to spend more time in schools explicitly focusing on understanding, composing, and sharing stories. Considering the prevalence of stories in education, why is storytelling not valued as much as other forms of communication in many classrooms?

Interrogating the Barriers to Storytelling in Schools

Three interrelated challenges stand in the way of storytelling gaining more traction as a tool for civic education and education writ large in schools today. First, there exists in our field a long-standing reluctance to acknowledge that the subject areas that structure secondary education (e.g., ELA, history, math, science) are not objective bodies of knowledge but rather subjective disciplinary narratives that privilege some concepts and perspectives and minimize others. The avalanche of standards, pacing calendars, and standardized testing makes it difficult for teachers to step back and recognize that our content areas are not apolitical but instead play a role in transmitting values and beliefs about our communities and the wider public sphere. If we fail to recognize the civic messages we are sending students through the stories of our content instruction, we contribute to the contracting of civic education to a narrow body of knowledge and skills and miss a powerful opportunity to inject civic learning into our daily practice.

What does it mean that our disciplines are structured by stories? For us as ELA teachers, it means recognizing that our subject area promotes particular understandings of what it means to be a so-called good reader, writer, listener, and speaker through the texts that often populate book rooms and the kinds of tasks that we ask students to perform to demonstrate their literacy skill. For instance, the fact that many required reading lists continue to feature a disproportionate number of white male authors, coupled with what we already know about how stories influence available perspectives on the world, leads to a situation in which a narrow range of experience represents the norm not only in who is considered a talented writer but also which societal views students encounter (Ebarvia et al., 2020).

Recognizing that our content area tells a story was a necessary first step for us to begin thinking about the stories we want our discipline to tell in order to match up with our overarching purpose of an equitable and justice-oriented civic future. Then we can take steps to adjust our curriculum and instruction accordingly. We ensured that the texts we introduced to students represented a range of authorial voices by deconstructing the idea of the canon and including multiple forms of expression from popular culture. We also sought to disrupt dominant ideas about what it means to be a competent writer.

The second challenge related to storytelling in schools is that across all school disciplines, students are largely encouraged to learn how to write and speak in the form of argument rather than story as preparation for college, career, and civic life. Standardized testing continues to have an outsized influence on content area instruction, so let's consider the types of writing that students are required to do on these exams. Besides perhaps one narrative writing exercise in ELA, the majority of prompts require expository, informational, or persuasive composition.

The rationale behind these exercises involves both giving students practice with the genres of writing they may encounter in the workplace and instilling the idea that informed argumentation represents the apex of deliberative dialogue in a democratic society. The particular focus on crafting arguments featuring claims and evidence has increased since the implementation of the Common Core State Standards, which has influenced literacy instruction across disciplines. The introduction to the Common Core ELA standards (National Governors Association, 2010) situates argument writing as necessary for "responsible citizenship in a democratic republic" (p. 3). As the standards were being rolled out across the country in 2011, one of the main organizers of the project, David Coleman, infamously told a group of educators that argument rather than narrative should be the focus of literacy instruction because "as you grow up in this world you realize people don't really give a shit about what you feel and what you think" (T F, 2012).

While this quote may involve a bit of tongue-in-cheek hyperbole, it does speak to the wider cultural assumption that storytelling is a soft creative skill whereas argumentation is a hard academic skill and that social and political decisions are made through the consideration of supposedly objective facts and evidence alone. As the neuroscience research discussed above has demonstrated, this is a reductive view; compelling stories about the nature and purpose of the society envisioned for the future can influence citizens just as much if not more than the facts marshaled to support particular policies. Additionally, the continued splintering of the media landscape has created a situation in which individuals can mistake the lies presented in disinformation as fact, making it impossible for conversation partners to agree on even a basic common starting point for dialogue.

The third challenge stifling storytelling in schools flows from the first two. Because stories are often submerged in both the structure and instructional priorities of our content areas, many teachers may feel unprepared to integrate storytelling into their practice. Storytelling is a vulnerable activity that taps into our identities, beliefs, and experiences at the deepest levels. It requires trust and the careful cultivation of humanizing connection. It weaves information into intricate narratives of who we were, who we are, and who we might yet become. These are not the qualities that mainstream models of schooling are built to develop, but they are the ones that our youth need in order to build compassionate and just futures. As a result, our practice must innovate. Let's explore how that can happen.

Innovating Our Commitment to Storytelling: Moving from Theory to Practice

Remember, you do not need to be an English Language Arts teacher to incorporate storytelling into your instruction. The reading, composing, and sharing of narratives can happen meaningfully across all disciplines and in response to any inquiries that students pose related to your subject area.

Let's return to the learning communities we have been following in order to consider three interrelated forms of civic storytelling that can enhance our commitment to world building in the classroom. These include: (1) individual, (2) interpersonal, and (3) community narratives. Of course, these three levels are always overlapping, but teasing them apart presents an opportunity for us to teach students about the ways that the ecosystems in our lives are always connected.

Telling Individual Stories

Once the Middle School 50 debate team decided to disrupt the fundamental structure of policy debate by rejecting the practice of arguing both for and against immigration restrictions—and instead asking participants in each round to imagine a borderless society with them—they were faced with another question. What would they actually say during their speeches to further this inquiry with the other team and the judge?

Coach Warren and the students knew that most teams spent their practices researching statistics and other information that they could use as evidence to support their claims. They had one folder each: one for the benefits and one for the dangers of loosening immigration restrictions. Hannah, one of the 8th-graders on the team, asked if they should simply collect more information about how immigrants contribute to society. But something didn't feel right. If their goal was to dream about a future in which borders did not exist, wouldn't sharing data justifying the worth of immigrants be contrary to that purpose?

The team needed a different approach, and they found one in storytelling. They first read the stories of authors who critiqued borders in their work. They saw how scholar Gloria Anzaldúa (1987) rejected the binaries created by borders not only through academic criticism but also through weaving poetry, personal narrative, and multiple languages into her writing. "I will have my voice," she said. The coaching team wondered what it would look like for poetry and personal experience to live within a debate round.

Before compiling any facts, the teachers enlisted the help of a spoken word poet to help the students weave their own immigration stories into their speeches. Eight of the 10 students on the team had either emigrated to the United States as children or were the children of immigrant parents. The storytelling felt a little weird at first. "I'll admit, at first I was like, is this even debate?" Alex, a 7th-grader, said, laughing. "But then I thought about my mom and how she could connect to this part of my speech because I was telling her story."

Students thought about how their stories might help the other students and adults in their debate round see that immigration is not an abstract topic to argue about, but rather a real part of their lives. Juan, an 8th-grader, wrote, "Leaving your country or the place where you were born is not always a choice you want to make. We do it because we are looking for a better future." Ofelia, a 7th-grader, praised the courage of her mother: "My mama was 18 when she came to America for a new opportunity . . . . Now is when we break down our borders. Now is when we come together and we form a new perspective."

Ana, an 8th-grader, wrote a poem integrating quotes, concepts, and styles from Anzaldúa's work to read at the start of each debate round:

> Yo hablo español
> My mom taught me to learn my beautiful Caribbean
>   language and
> I'm proud
> Por eso voy a debatir hoy en mis dos lenguajes
> As long as I have to accommodate the English speakers rather

than having them accommodate me, my tongue will be
  illegitimate.
They look at me with xenophobic eyes,
Is it true?
That my mom is illegitimate
I am illegitimate
My eyes
My words
My thoughts
My curves
My partner
My team
Are we illegitimate? Am I?
I speak in words of power that no one could imagine even
  pronouncing a word in,
I speak a different language,
AM I ILEGAL?

The storytelling practice of MS 50's debate team developed in response to their inquiry and demonstrates the power of individual narrative to enrich both the disciplinary content of their learning about immigration and the potential composition structures they could use to express that learning in ways that pushed against the boundaries of a traditional academic argument exercise. The team did not reject information and argumentation altogether; instead, they made the conscious choice to begin civic dialogue with personal storytelling in order to change the stakes of the discussion from one of distanced, so-called objective policy options to urgent and immediate human concern.

Each of us has disciplinary content and composition structures to work with in our subject areas. This means we have the necessary conditions to elicit personal stories from our students to make what we teach relevant, engaging, and authentic in the civic world they inhabit outside of the classroom. When we organize our classes around the practice of inquiry and welcome the juicy questions that students bring related to our disciplines, their stories will not be far behind. Here are some strategies for cultivating them.

Getting Started: Autoethnography. The stories of the MS 50 debate team were powerful because they served two purposes simultaneously. First, they validated and celebrated the personal lives and literacy practices of students and their families. Second, they connected students' individual experiences to broader academic and social contexts—in this case, the academic exercise of debate and the public issue of immigration. Both of these purposes are crucial in their own right; the combination embodies the transformative power of civic storytelling.

Civic storytelling goes beyond the getting-to-know-you activities that often occur during the first few weeks of the school year, although these activities are super important as the foundation for culturally sustaining and student-centered pedagogy. Civic storytelling makes an explicit and intentional linkage between individuals and the overlapping communities to which those individuals belong. We like to explain this nuance to students by differentiating two storytelling practices: autobiography and autoethnography.

In autobiography, the focus leans toward the individual; interpretation and analysis are of course present, but the goal is to zero in on a personal life story. In autoethnography, the explicit focus involves analyzing individual experience within cultural context. Autoethnography originates from the Greek roots ethno- (race, people, or culture) and -graphy (writing) and now refers to a research methodology involving the systematic and detailed study of how people make sense of the world within particular social communities (Richardson, 1994).

When introducing these terms to the middle school debaters, coauthor Nicole put it this way. An autobiographical prompt would ask: What is your immigration story? An autoethnographic prompt asks: How does your immigration story reflect and extend the understandings and assumptions about immigration reflected in media, public policy, and political discourse? The autoethnographic lens helps students to recognize that each of our unique individual stories are inescapably linked to broader social and civic issues.

You can support students to engage in autoethnography by first designing activities that show students how your academic subject area matters within the real world and is reflected in their individual lives. These connections are made in some subject areas more easily than others; for example, history teachers can draw pretty explicit linkages between past and current events and trace the impact of broad historical shifts on the specific family histories of students. For math teachers, it may take a bit more work to tease out the social uses of math and show students how it is used to justify particular policies or contribute to narratives that affect the lived experience of communities.

Doing this design work demonstrates to students the civic importance of every class period of the day. It gives an authentic response to the question, "Why are we learning this?" Once you share an ethnographic analysis of your subject area with students, you are then poised to ask your students to compose autoethnographies from their perspective. How do they see the experiences of their lives intersecting with the fundamental narratives and tensions of your discipline? Offering students this lens early in your courses alongside a focus on inquiry sets the tone for sustained civic learning in every element of instruction.

We have worked with a wide range of students to compose autoethnographies, from middle schoolers to preservice teacher candidates. These stories need not be in traditional written form; in fact, we like to encourage students to use multiple modalities (e.g., images, video, art) to express themselves because it invites creativity and it expands definitions of what stories can be. We also often ask students to bring physical artifacts to class to share with their peers alongside or as part of their narratives in order to build community and ground abstract concepts in material form.

Taking It to the Next Level: Disrupting Disciplinary Norms. The MS 50 debate team strategically employed civic storytelling in order to expose the arbitrary rules governing policy debate discourse and agitate for a more expansive range of acceptable ways to talk about current events. As discussed previously, each of our disciplines require students to write in particular genres in order to express their knowledge and skills. ELA has essays, History has document-based questions, Math has proofs, and so on. Once we have delved into the practice of autoethnography with our students and unearthed the narratives that undergird our subject area, we can then begin to innovate the very structures of our disciplines.

We encourage a mindset of pragmatic idealism: the idea that we as teachers should dream big and then adapt those dreams to the constraints of our contexts rather than allowing the existing systems in which we teach to preemptively reduce the size of our goals. That mindset applies here as we consider the extent to which we can disrupt the disciplinary norms of our classes. As ELA teachers, we did not feel comfortable completely discarding the genre of the five-paragraph essay, much as we wanted to, because we knew that our students needed to demonstrate mastery of this form on the standardized tests that would have very real consequences for their academic trajectories. But because we refused to allow our classes to shrink to fit the forms of these tests, we ensured that our units always culminated in a second and more valued assessment that offered students opportunities to play with different narrative forms.

Rather than only write an argument essay, students might create a Twitter thread (complete with memes) to persuade their followers of their claims. Rather than only write a text-based creative story, students might produce a short film to screen at a community showcase. If we want our students to share our belief that the education they receive at school is preparing them to build the future they desire and deserve, we need to bend our disciplines toward authentic civic ends rather than asking students to bend to the often-outdated norms of those disciplines.

What forms of writing are prevalent in your subject area and what alternative forms could demonstrate similar skills with a creative touch (see Table 4.2)?

Table 4.2   Disciplinary Writing Alternatives

YOUR SUBJECT AREA/CLASS:	
Traditional Writing Genres	*Creative Alternatives*

Telling Interpersonal Stories

The teachers were frustrated. They wanted the Digital Democratic Dialogue (3D) Project to be a learning community in which
students from different communities could talk with each other
about controversial social issues with a level of compassion and
empathy that was in such short supply among many adults in
public life. When the teachers launched the online discussion
platform and organized students into cross-school groups based
on their chosen topics, the teachers urged everyone to learn from
each other rather than argue or seek to persuade anyone of their
perspective. It wasn't starting out so well.

During a team meeting, the teachers read the posts from
one group focused on gun reform as an example. From the very
beginning, it seemed like the students had internalized the idea
that every conversation about current events must involve argument. Brandon, a student from California, introduced himself
by saying, "Hello everyone, I will be joining you in this debate."
John, a student from Texas, shared a statistic he found from a
database: "We lose eight children and teenagers to gun violence every day." Brandon countered with evidence from his own
research: "There have been more deaths in 2017, 2018, and 2019
from strokes, Alzheimer's disease, diabetes, and kidney disease."

After students traded these talking points, the conversation
fizzled out. The teachers marveled at how much the persuasive
essay format seeped into student conversation and the difference
between a successful essay and a successful conversation. How
could they get students to move beyond the talking points?

They decided to remind students to share their personal stories rather than immediately turning to information sources. They
asked them to explain why the issue they had chosen mattered
to them and how it showed up in their lives. When responding to
other students' posts, the teachers advised them to draw upon
what they called "the 4 C's"—care, connection, community, and
curiosity—to build trust and keep dialogue flowing.

When the team returned to the gun reform group two weeks
later, they saw progress. Marcus, a student from Pennsylvania,
posted, "Gun violence is very important to me because I lost

three people 'cause of it this summer. The gun problem is getting out of hand in my neighborhood." Brandon, instead of responding with a talking point, shared his personal perspective: "My beliefs about guns have to come from my family which have been hunting their whole lives 'til this day and would tell me when they were my age they would have their rifles on the back of their truck so when school got out they would go hunting and not have to worry about anyone shooting the school."

These posts sparked further conversation rather than diminishing it. Marcus told Brandon that he had never hunted before and Brandon replied, "Do you have any questions about hunting or guns that I could answer?" Marcus posted, "Yeah, I do have a few questions. What guns do you use? When did you start?" Other students in the group jumped in to share their experiences and ask questions. The teachers reported that their students were coming to them after class to share how interesting it was to learn about how other teenagers thought.

Christina, the teacher from Pennsylvania, noticed that Marcus became much more engaged by the project through his interactions with Brandon. She explained, "There was something about it being authentic that allowed him to say to me, 'That's so different than my experience. I don't really understand that, but I want to get into it.'"

The teachers and students of the 3D Project quickly realized that composing an argument involves a different skill set than communicating with actual human beings. Perhaps students were receiving too much instruction geared toward the former and not enough toward the latter. While developing claims, gathering evidence, and weighing alternatives are all important civic skills, they do not exist in a vacuum; the core of public life involves interpersonal communication. Social change does not proceed only through debate; it gathers steam when community members learn each other's stories and develop a common vision.

So many of the ways that we ask students to demonstrate their learning in schools focus upon individual effort. Making the choice to consciously cultivate the skills needed to support empathetic interpersonal communication is a way to manifest commitment to civic learning. Doing so through the practice of storytelling advances the goals of equity, justice, and agency by fostering vulnerable and humanizing connections between students. Let's consider ways to get students sharing with each other, first within your classroom and then beyond it.

Getting Started: Stance or Values Dialogues.   When Marcus and Brandon first began talking to each other in their 3D Project discussion group, they staked out contrasting arguments about guns: Marcus was in favor of gun control measures while Brandon opposed them. Because of their assumption that discussion of civic issues necessarily implied debate, and because they associated debate with the academic practices of citing evidence from information sources and avoiding personal experience, they began trading statistics. It wasn't until they stepped back to interrogate the stories that informed their arguments and seriously considered each other's perspectives that they reached a deeper level of understanding and connection from which further civic deliberation could occur. Their actions encourage us to ask questions of our own practice: Do we communicate assumptions about argument in the projects we assign our students? How do we unearth the stories that lie beneath those claims as the foundation for more productive dialogue?

We have already discussed the necessary first step of giving students space to tease out their personal relationships to topics without the immediate drive to make arguments about them. The next steps involve supporting them to (1) uncover the values they hold dear as a result of their experiences; (2) consider how those values inform the positions they take on public issues; and (3) negotiate how to respond when encountering others who may prioritize different values. A discussion that starts from a place of sharing values has the potential to be much more productive and compassionate than one that starts from a place of staking claims.

Consider how Marcus and Brandon's personal storytelling helped them shift away from claims and toward a deeper consideration of values. Marcus' story about losing loved ones to gun violence contributed to his desire for reform measures by tapping into his value of collective safety, whereas Brandon's association of guns with family and recreation reflected the value he placed on individual responsibility and choice. Obviously, values are not so clear-cut; they are overlapping and contradictory and shifting. Neither Marcus nor Brandon believe in just one value. By sharing stories with each other, they began to realize that they could not simply discount or rebut each other's perspectives as they could with their statistics; they had to think seriously about how people can manage competing values while living together in good faith.

It is often difficult to recognize the values informing pro/con positions, let alone talk about them with others when activities like debates and persuasive essays jump straight into claims and evidence. One activity to help create that bridge between stories and arguments is to engage students in what we call stance dialogues. Much like what occurred in the 3D Project, the stance dialogue revolves around a topic about which individuals often have differing opinions. The participants come to the dialogue with the goal of communicating not the argument they want to make about the topic, but the stance they take toward it based on the values they prioritize.

Table 4.3 offers a way for students to both organize their own thinking and take notes about what they learn from their dialogue partners. It does not need to be used in a linear way; students may start from an argument or claim they believe in and work their way backwards to excavate the values that inform it or tell a story related to a topic and forge their stances and arguments from there. You can provide students with a word bank of potential values and discuss them or have students add their own.

Table 4.3   Story, Stance, and Argument

TOPIC:		
Story	Stance/Values	Argument
Potential values related to civic life: safety, security, individual choice, collective responsibility, freedom, diversity, fairness, _____ , _____ .		

Once students determine their stances and values, discussions can grapple with the extent to which those values can coexist in a community dedicated to the overarching commitments of equity and justice. Before every discussion, students can use the 4 C's as a guide for responding to their peers.

4 C'S

Care: Show appreciation for how your partner shared something personal about themselves. You can do that by explaining how much a specific part of what your partner said helped you to learn something about them.

Connection: Maybe you share the experiences or ideas of your partner. Maybe you couldn't be more different. But you likely can find some point of connection where something your partner said affected you.

Community: We all have unique locations and ideas, but we are part of overlapping communities. What is your partner making you think about in terms of what a common civic future could look like?

Curiosity: What do you want to ask your partner to keep your conversation going?

These dialogues do not come to neat conclusions, but they do help students see behind pro/con binaries and recognize that debates over controversial issues are really struggles of people to determine how to live together amid differences in a spirit of common cause.

Taking It to the Next Level: Building Dialogue Networks. Stance dialogues can offer the students in your classes the opportunity to forge deeper and more trusting relationships with each other. They can also help students see the range of experiences, stances, and arguments that can exist within a single school community. Once you have developed a culture of communication within your classroom, you can begin to consider ways to widen the circle further. One of the most powerful elements of the 3D Project was the cross-school connection, which enabled students to gain a window into the lives of peers living in different contexts. With whom could you connect your students?

You may be prepared to reach out to far-flung colleagues and utilize digital media tools to link your students, but meaningful dialogue can also occur on a smaller scale closer to home. We both taught in large districts in which the demographics of the student population varied greatly from school to school with regard to race, socioeconomic status, political affiliations, and more. The persistence of residential and school segregation within the United States creates a situation in which students who live within a relatively small geographic area could have very different experiences and civic identities. Consider forging relationships with schools within your district or perhaps your region. Facilitating conversations across grade levels could also be generative.

Remember that young people are not the only ones with stories to share. Connections with families, after-school providers, community organizations, local business or faith leaders, and more could all be tapped to engage in storytelling and dialogue. The more perspectives that students encounter and the more opportunities they have to consider the identities, values, and dreams of their fellow community members, the better prepared they will be to approach public problems with a spirit of critical civic empathy. We'll discuss the value of such networks further in the next chapter.

Telling Community Stories

As their peers at Manual Arts High School planned their teacher workshops, the Roosevelt High School students from the Council of Youth Research wrestled with which direction to take their inquiry. They couldn't help noticing the chatter around the building from their teachers and administrators about a recently released documentary film that called out their school by name. The film was called *Waiting for Superman*. Its poster depicted a student in a school uniform sitting at a desk, hand raised, amid a scene of apocalyptic destruction; the tagline read, "The fate of

our country won't be decided on a battlefield. It will be determined in a classroom."

When students watched the film, they saw that it followed
several students from across the country as they sought to gain
acceptance to charter schools in a bid to brighten their future
prospects. The film's argument, as they saw it, was that students
needed heroes to whisk them away from their failing neighborhood schools if they wanted to succeed. And one of the
neighborhood schools featured as a failure was their own.

During conversations in their after-school meetings, the Roosevelt students thought about the number of people who would
watch that film and without any further information or context
pass judgment upon their school and their community. The film
used test scores and graduation rates to tell Roosevelt's story.
The students had seen articles in the local paper that took a similar approach. They chafed at the idea that these statistics painted
an incomplete portrait. What about the lack of funding that pre-
vented the school from offering more services? What about the
turnover of administrators each year that fostered continuing
instability? Most importantly, what about the generations of students, families, and teachers who cared deeply about Roosevelt
and worked tirelessly to improve it?

The students realized that if they wanted members of their
community to see past the one-dimensional portrayal of their
school that was so often presented in mainstream media, they
were the ones in the best position to tell a more nuanced story.
They decided to focus their inquiry on shifting the narrative
about Roosevelt by telling stories of assets rather than deficits.
They would talk to their teachers, classmates, and community
leaders—the people who knew Roosevelt best.

As Maria told her group, "We don't need superheroes to come
and save us. We are our own superheroes."

The Roosevelt High School students recognized that stories have
immense power to shape perceptions of entire communities and public
issues, particularly when they are composed by individuals from social

groups with social and political power and disseminated in mass media outlets. But although some stories dominate the public imagination, they do not hold a monopoly on truth or accuracy. Once the students realized that each individual story has affordances and constraints, they understood the need for more stories to disrupt dominant narratives and reveal the multifaceted nature of complicated issues.

As students are invited to share more individual and interpersonal stories, their understanding of the overlapping communities in their lives can expand along with their capacity to question assumptions and critique partial narratives. These abilities are essential to naming and challenging inequities and creating futures in which the stories of those closest to civic challenges are amplified and honored. Consuming and creating counter-narratives that address long-standing tensions or absences in your discipline can start students on this path.

Getting Started: Recognizing Media Tropes. Through their own self-reflection and conversations with others, the Roosevelt students came to identify several communities that mattered to them, including their school, their neighborhood, and the wider identity group of young people at large. Once they identified these communities and sought to explore how they were represented within their inquiry area of education, they realized that the media often communicated simplistic narratives about them that robbed them of their complexity and nuance. The documentary transmitted messages to them that their school was a failure, their neighborhood was a wasteland, and adults know better than young people. Identifying the stock narratives, or tropes, that formed the basis of stereotypes and public opinion allowed students to deconstruct and then challenge them with their own counter-narratives.

As your students name the important communities in their own lives and make connections between those communities, their inquiry interests, and civic life, the tools of critical media analysis can help students discover the role that rhetoric, bias, and even misinformation can play in civic decision making. The Roosevelt students recognized that when their school was framed as a failure in news reports, it made it easier for some policy makers to argue that funding and resources should be allocated to other schools rather than used to improve their own. How do your students see people like them—however they choose to define themselves—being represented in the media? What impacts do these media narratives have in society?

Calls for digital media literacy in school have grown louder amid a recognition of the overwhelming amount of information that we all encounter online. Oftentimes it is treated as an add-on to content-area instruction and involves isolated exercises asking students to distinguish fact from opinion or a trustworthy news source from a biased one. Integrating media into your class in a way that instead ties authentically into the stories and topics that students already care about can make media literacy a more civically relevant practice.

MEDIA ANALYSIS QUESTIONS

1. What story is this piece of media telling about my topic?
2. How is my community framed within this story?
3. How could this story influence public opinion about my topic and my community?
4. Where are the silences or gaps in this story? Whose perspectives are not present?
5. What questions do I need to explore next?

Taking It to the Next Level: Community Counter-Narratives. Once students identify untold stories living in the shadows of dominant media narratives about their communities, they can begin to compose and disseminate their own counter-narratives as a way to exert their civic agency. The Roosevelt students engaged in inquiry in their school by asking their friends, families, and teachers to share their stories about the role of education in their lives; they then wove those stories together into a multimedia presentation they could share in a local showcase and on social media to creatively speak back to those who would seek to define their community for them rather than with them.

Brainstorm with your students how they can respond to media portrayals with which they take issue. The "letter to the editor" genre has now exploded with a range of social media options that students can leverage to get their voices heard. TikTok videos, Instagram Live broadcasts, teach-ins, and more open the door of possibility for your students. They will likely develop ideas you could never have dreamt up on your own. Again, when you plan these inquiry and storytelling opportunities to intentionally live within your disciplinary curriculum, you can simultaneously ensure that students gain content-area knowledge and skill while advocating for the social futures they desire.

Survival Through Story

"To survive, you must tell stories."

—Umberto Eco (2006)

In the previous chapter, we described asking questions as a civic act. We now add telling stories as well. Injecting the creativity and compassion of storytelling into the journey to craft a shared future on the streets of our neighborhoods and across this fragile planet reminds us that at its core, civic education is not about policies, procedures, and structures. It is about the drive for each of us to enjoy individual and collective agency within a just and humanizing society. As Eco reminds us, we need stories to make it through the trials and tribulations of a troubled world. Narratives remind us that despite our differences, we are inextricably linked. Through our classroom practice, we can support students to recognize both the power that dominant stories have to influence our assumptions about the world and the possibilities opened up by counter-storytelling to disrupt the status quo and create new plotlines for the future.

Discussion Questions

1. What are the stories that structure your discipline or subject area? What values and beliefs are being transmitted to students about public life through these stories?
2. How could you alter your content and instruction to offer alternative stories to students that support the goals you have for their civic futures?

3. What opportunities exist in your classroom for students to tell their stories? How can you create more invitations for storytelling?
4. Who could you forge connections with in your school, local community, and wider social network to offer students authentic opportunities to share stories that will expand their civic perspectives?

Chapter 5

Building the Future Through
Civic Networking

In a meeting with a handful of other civic education researchers, our colleague, Joel Westheimer, made an observation in passing: "Fifty percent of social justice is *social*" (personal communication, 2013). With a playful truism, Westheimer reminded us that some of what is necessary in order to do the hard work of organizing, of collaborating, and of working toward goals that might at times look ludicrous to others and impossible to ourselves is a healthy dose of laughter, trust, and companionship. We do not meet the complex goal of making a future brighter and freer through individual hard work and old-fashioned elbow grease, as much as some of us might try. Transformative change, as we imagine it across these chapters, is about so much more than the ideas and actions of individuals. We are hoping our students, our colleagues, and we ourselves are committed to social change along the lines of what Westheimer mentions.

If there is a social element to striving toward justice (and we agree with Westheimer that there is), we must be savvy about how we plan for collaboration and determine whom we interact with, learn from, and build with. We must be intentional about our networking practices. Like Westheimer's emphasis on the social aspect of social justice, we want to focus this chapter on the "work" component of networking. Building allyship, solidarity, and mutually aligned movements (all within standards-aligned classrooms, no less) is hard work. It requires compromises, it requires adjusting power relationships in classrooms, and it requires the kinds of "patient impatience" that Paulo Freire (2005) describes as fundamental to the task at hand.

As we consider civic networking practices within classrooms, this chapter focuses on three kinds of networking orientations that students and teachers should interrogate and innovate around (see Table 5.1). In particular, after detailing some of the basic concepts and practices of networking, we argue for starting with approaches to linking students in your classrooms closer together; that is, networking within your classroom context. Next, we explore expansive networking possibilities outside of the walls of your classrooms. Finally, we consider how our networking practices must proactively work toward liberatory transformation, thus, networking toward future possibilities.

Table 5.1 Interrogating and Innovating with Networking

NETWORKING LENS	WHAT TO INTERROGATE	TOOLS TO INNOVATE
Networking Within	1. What expertise is present in our classrooms? 2. How are students and our colleagues collaborating and working toward shared goals?	Classroom Network Mapping Democratic Classroom Roles
Networking Beyond	1. What are the shared interests and desires that might lead toward collaboration? 2. Who are the local and virtual contacts we can connect with?	Critical Issue Exploration Community Walks and Asset Mapping
Networking Toward Freedom	1. How are we in dialogue with the movements of our ancestors? 2. What predigital technologies can we utilize in our work moving forward?	Expanding Networks into the Not-Yet

What Is Networking and Why Does It Matter?

When considering networking in today's world, we often initially imagine the kinds of complex algorithmic social networks that bring together people online. These are important elements of what we will discuss throughout this chapter, but they are something of an endpoint or a single node in the long line of networked practices across the grand scope of human development. As social animals, humans inherently connect, play, and collaborate with one another. It is in our nature, and it is how we learn, grow, and innovate. Networking as we conceptualize it includes all of these processes of connecting with others and extending what we are capable of doing by extending whom we do things with.

Navigating a Digital Democracy

We've hinted that technology drives many of the ways people today network and imagine what networking looks like. However, before we fully dive into the practices of civic networking, we'd like to offer a caveat about technology's role. Perhaps, like many of us, when you saw the word networking at the beginning of this book and this chapter you implicitly attached the word social to it. Your mind conjured the platforms that mediate much of our social and civic lives today: Facebook, Instagram, and whatever new series of apps and digital resources our students are connected on these days. While there is tremendous potential for these platforms to be leveraged for civic networking, we want to recognize that they are but one part of a larger suite of civic networking practices.

While these social networks and digital tools can help shift the dimensions of what seems possible in our classroom, we do not want to limit this chapter's discussion simply to digital tools created by non-educator entrepreneurs that center profit. Instead, we center people in our networking efforts throughout this chapter. The tools will change but, fundamentally, we need to instill practices that allow us to collaborate and draw out the best in one another. If we are building a safety net for our society, the work we are doing is with each other.

At the same time that we center people, we are not ignorant of the ways digital platforms—such as social networking companies like Facebook, Instagram, and Twitter—have altered where and how digital discourse transpires. We have spent substantial aspects of our scholarly and teaching work exploring the civic demands of learning, participating, and pushing against political discourse that often occurs on these platforms. From their substantive role in recent U.S. presidential elections to the uplifting ways savvy youth leverage these tools for localized change and organizing, democratic participation in the United States and elsewhere often relies on the digital tools that mediate many aspects of our daily lives today. At the same time, these tools are constantly changing. The Silicon Valley companies, the apps that are in fashion, and the verbs we might use to describe searching, viewing, and annotating online material as part of our digitally networked lives are in a constant and dizzying flux. Instead of suggesting that teachers must stay abreast of the latest electronic gadgets, we suggest focusing on the contexts of what matters the most; this extends on our previous work (e.g., Philip & Garcia, 2015), that considers youth expertise and the digital ecosystem of today's schools.

Although this chapter assumes we will utilize digital tools to strengthen aspects of our civic networking practices, we approach this assumption with an understanding that these tools must come secondary to human-powered possibilities. As researchers who have leveraged the powerful possibilities of social media and social networks for classroom learning, we want to recognize the very harmful practices that they have perpetuated for too long as well. In October 2021, a Facebook whistleblower, Frances Haugen, shared a bevy of damning information about Facebook and Instagram's profit-over-people practices (Timberg, 2021). Most troubling to us were the ways that Facebook knowingly suppressed research that some teen girls' suicidal thoughts increased after using Instagram or that, in one study, 17% of teen girls felt their eating disorders became more severe after social media use (Timberg, 2021). These leaks point not only to the damning effects that emerge from the norms of existing social media platforms but also to the insidious role that these companies play in actively harming the most vulnerable members of society—all in the name of profit and user acquisition. We urge an abundance of levelheaded caution when relying on digital tools for humanistic purposes.

Innovating Our Commitment to Networking: Moving from Theory to Practice

One important note we want to make before we move forward: It is imperative to recognize that this chapter is not about establishing networking practices for simply bettering student classroom experiences. This chapter extends the principles of networking in two directions: It moves outwardly to include the purposes and contexts of networking beyond classroom walls, and it moves across traditional classroom hierarchies. Teachers need to be considered a part of learning networks, not just facilitating them. In fact, as we explore in our continuing description of the 3D project, networks of teachers are a fundamental aspect of how we push for democratizing the educational possibilities of our classrooms. When we use networking tools and practices to intentionally improve our work as teachers, we can "coconstruct new forms of meaning and understanding in ways that are individually and collectively valuable and apply that knowledge in their professional practice" (Booth & Kellogg, 2015). Rather than thinking about networks as ties that link one group of students with another, we hope this chapter leaves you invigorated to expand the contexts of how learning is transformed across space and time for students, for adults, and for the broad ecosystem of individuals committed to justice. Frankly, while we might on our best days do a good job of interrogating the lessons of past activist movements, we have largely ignored the possibilities of understanding how to network through and with historical movements in our efforts to better our designs for the future.

Networking Within

In the final weeks of the Black Cloud game, students had collected myriad real-world data about the air quality in their neighborhood and school. They had communicated with a fictitious cloud and constructed a narrative to imagine how to mitigate pollution. Imagination and data collided on a daily basis and it was time for the students to get their hands dirty. Literally.

As a culminating task, students were split into two groups to imagine environmentally sustainable cities of the future ("ecotopias"). This activity required foraging, designing, and articulating specific and ideologically grounded visions of environmental actions in the future. It was messy work that saw more than a dozen students working in closely synchronized activities. In order to accomplish this work, coauthor Antero worked with several colleagues to develop unique roles for every student. Some of these were playfully silly and mirrored a slightly sardonic tone for the game. However, rather than imagine discrete, individual roles, this project had students collaborate as part of a unique set of conglomerations named after various systems found within the body that must all work together for each of us to thrive. A substantial portion of these roles and the task assignment follow below, as an example of how networking within your own classroom might play out.

Imagine an ecotopian city. Here steam power runs everything, instead of gasoline power and electricity. What does your city run on? How do people and goods move around? Is the city dystopian or utopian? Do tourists like to visit? Does the city create much pollution? Does it generate much heat? Discuss these questions with your team. Using the tools provided and found materials, build a model of your Ecopolis and prepare to take Pufftron sensor measurements. May the cleaner, brighter city win!

Every citizen of every community has a role to play. Communities rely on people doing their part: teachers, garbage collectors, doctors, lawyers, parents, children, and so on. What role(s) do you play in your community? Today, you get a new role in a new city. This city doesn't exist yet. With everyone working together, using all our information and all our resources, we will build it from scratch.

There will be two cities: one by First Breath and one by Xylon. Just like real cities, they are separate but learn and grow by watching each other. There are 5 systems, 15 roles, and 15 resources. These roles are just our idea of how a city works. Your ideas may be different and that is fine.

CIRCULATORY SYSTEM

Merchant: Recyclables.   Things, things, things, people love to own things! Our things define who we are. The Merchant finds the things the city is made of. They coordinate the finding and collecting of material, like interesting trash from the streets and homes. They must also make sure this trash is safe (i.e., no sharp parts), nontoxic (ask for help if needed), and non-gross!

IMMUNE SYSTEM

Surgeon General: Fans.   Nothing keeps the Black Cloud at bay like good, fresh air! Since we don't have wind in the classroom, we have to make it ourselves. The Surgeon General makes sure the Pufftron breathes fresh air and that air flows well through the city. They are also responsible for monitoring and reducing any and all pollutants.

Media: Journal.   Newspapers, television, radio, internet: It's how we learn about the world, but it's also how the world learns about us! The Media are in charge of telling the world about their city. They keep a written record of events and decisions in the building of the Ecopolis. They work closely with The Artist, The Scholar, and The Tourist.

Tourist: Camera.   Nothing teaches you more about your city than visiting another city! The Tourist is allowed to visit the other Ecopolis at any time, as long as accompanied by that city's official tour guide, The Jester. They also take photos and video of the other team's city and present them to The Media.

NERVOUS SYSTEM

Artist: Paint.   Art is the mirror of every society. It shows us how beautiful we are and how ugly we can be. The Artist ensures the ecotopia is visually pleasing using paint, collage, etc. They also create drawings for the Media and the Prophet when needed.

SKELETAL SYSTEM

Biologist: Clay.   Biology is the science of life. Every city is built on and from the Earth, and must always be aware of the life that grows within and around them. The Biologist creates the terrain of the city with clay and other materials. They also work with The Matriarch to place and water the plants.

Engineer: Tools. Math, physics, biology, art: Engineers have to think of everything! The Engineer is in charge of measuring and cutting all materials. They work with The Prophet in zoning the city, making sure everything is in the right place and that nothing has been left out.

Understandably, these roles will not be the ones you use in your own classroom. This likely looks different from the group roles that you have been taught to implement in your classroom—maybe even a bit wacky. But that's the point. What does it mean to intentionally shift our expectations of what a role in a classroom can look like or feel like? How might you reimagine your classroom interactions if students realign their relationships in wildly different kinds of networks?

Getting Started: Classroom Network Mapping. Give every student a chance to participate. Make sure the roles and responsibilities are rotated amongst students. Ensure students all have equal voice in how an assignment is completed.

These are the seemingly benign approaches to engaging young people in collaboration in our classrooms. We have all utilized these kinds of tenets in how we design student interactions with their peers, and, on the surface, these probably feel like the right designs. However, when it comes to building camaraderie and teamwork in our classrooms— building an authentic network of students who learn to rely on and trust one another—these guiding principles ultimately undercut what we aspire to achieve. This is because the approaches to collaboration in our classrooms do little to center trust, expertise, or student interests. Instead, we have conditioned students to numbly interact without establishing stakes around why we are participating or without providing meaningful outlets for expression in this work. What's worse, these approaches can reinforce a myth of meritocracy that allows some students to grasp the reins of group work, take the lead, and demonstrate a school-based mastery that instills confidence in those few students at the expense of their peers'.

Like many of the instructional practices we have been taught to deploy in our classrooms, the approaches we've tended to create for integrating group work are often framed as apolitical and given the veneer of equity: Everybody should do their part and, if we just try hard enough, our efforts will lead to success. But we need to interrogate the kinds of lessons we are instilling in young people by endorsing these approaches to group work. At best these are functioning multicultural depictions of kumbaya that obscure the racialized, gendered, and class-based practices that have cleaved civic opportunity for too long. They let those students that thrive at systems of schooling continue to do so and give easy exit routes for the students disinclined (or actively discouraged in some cases) to participate.

At the time that we are writing this, a popular meme is frequently circulating amongst educators differentiating equity and equality by showing different individuals trying to look over a fence at a baseball game. The "equal" participants all have the same sized crates, meaning the shortest individual is still unable to see the in-progress game. In comparison, an equitable distribution of these crates means that the taller individual forgoes their crate so that everyone has an opportunity to see what is transpiring. Of course, this model of differentiation is worthy of critique as well: Why does a fence exist in the first place and why is there a limit to the kinds of crates? The binary distinction between equal and equitable represented in the meme gets to the core of why models of group work that fail to account for the individuals in our classroom will always fall short.

So, let us be very clear: The democratic models of teamwork that create healthy classroom cultures are, of course, important practices. We do not mean to diminish the important ways students learn to collaborate with one another in classrooms. Yet, when the stakes of networking and working together are arbitrary participation points in a classroom, it is little wonder that familiar dynamics of unengaged students dragging each other toward tepid finish lines feels unfulfilling for all involved.

What can you do? Obviously, we don't mean to throw group work in the garbage bin. On the contrary, we want to offer two concrete steps to innovate the networking possibilities within your classroom. Together, these steps allow us to look at the process that gets students into group work in the first place and then refocuses that time around play, interest, and expertise. First, we need to recognize that every successful learning interaction is based on relationships and shared interests. How can we ask students to do more than arbitrary tasks together if we haven't cultivated a sense of who they are and what they are interested in?

You don't need fancy tools to understand your students. Rather, what would it look like for you to create a classroom network map of student interests and expertise? First, start by asking students to describe more of their backgrounds and interests. If you don't have a process for this kind of work at the beginning of your year, some sample prompts could include:

- What are two communities that are important to you? Why?
- What is something that is personally interesting to you?
- What are two things you are exceptionally good at that most people might not know about you?
- When you get the opportunity to help other people, what do you think is one of your strongest personal attributes?

To be explicit, these questions are not the ones you hand out to students at minute one of the first day of class. Rather, your classroom community will need to share a common understanding of what a "community" means. Is your school a community? If your classroom aspires to be a loving community, what will it take? Getting to these questions will let your students understand their role in a flourishing democratic space.

Now that you've developed a sense of letting students take inventory of their interests and strengths, you might next develop a map for students to build links across these different interests. One way we've seen this happen in classrooms is for students to create a paper with keywords of their interests and strengths or maybe an icon or logo to represent themselves, if some of your learners are graphically inclined.

With our 3D Project classrooms, students were able to peruse their community stories through online posts. Those technologies might get in the way when everyone is in the same room so you could instead have students rotate through your classroom to see and understand each other's expertise. You can frame this as a gallery walk with students offering sticky notes of affirmations and suggested resources based on what students created. Depending on the time you invest in this activity, you might have students collectively cluster similar interests and queries or you might do this on your own as a preparatory tool for your own instructional needs; might you all draw a map of what the terrain of expertise and interest in your classroom looks like? Either way, the hope would be that this activity allows you to see a clearer topology of what kinds of skills and interests must be uncovered and leveraged in your classroom.

As with every activity in this book, this is not something we believe is anchored to a grade level or to a subject area. Every teacher should be getting to know their students. If your students share the same teachers, stretching this networked mapping activity across multiple classes increases the opportunities for students to feel affirmed and engaged in their learning.

Taking It to the Next Level: Democratic Classroom Roles. Once you have started the process of getting to know your students and their interests—and once you've shared your own interests with the class— we use this information as a foundation for guiding how networking and collaboration are enacted. All that not-so-great group work you're trying to avoid? That's built on assignments and projects that are not responsive to or designed around the unique contexts of your classroom. Your civically transformative classroom is built on the recognition that these personal relationships and the individual students and their brilliance are what matter. So, we need to use this foundation as exactly that: The answers to pedagogical guidance are not hiding in the back of someone else's textbook or on a handout shared in your recent mandated professional development. Rather than rote assignments that require predetermined outcomes, we need to actually use the investment developed in your classroom. If you know what students think they are good at and what they want to learn more about, that is your starting place.

It is time for us to address a simple truth about networking and having students work together in our classrooms today. There's a not-so-dirty secret about group work in classrooms: it's usually not very effective. If we're being honest, there is a lot of learning time wasted and the typical roles for group work mean that students end up doing tasks they don't like doing in ways that do not challenge them. As adults, we can understand this; why would we try hard to achieve something that does not feel meaningful to us and that does not have a clear kind of reward attached to it? We recognize that it takes time and energy to produce assignments that students might care about. Even then, this work might fall flat. These are the kinds of investments we make as educators. It may feel like a stretch to connect a student's interests in skateboarding or ocean life with the given history or mathematics project in front of you. However, you will find that dialogue with students and a willingness to rethink the connections that students make will eventually help us get toward something productive. This is work that gets easier over time and our current approaches to curriculum design—reproducing existing assignments—often get in the way of the intellectual genius we have developed as responsive educators.

Unfortunately, group work is often set up to emphasize the completion of rote and task-oriented work rather than the dynamics of supporting and cultivating a meaningful group. This could probably be offered as a meta-reflection on most classroom dynamics, as well. Aside from the work of building affirming and trusting relationships to drive useful contexts of group work, we must center the identities and interests of the individuals in a group.

The typical roles we assign to students may seem useful in that they describe the work that needs to be completed. However, they do not spark imagination or push students beyond the predefined limits of narrow tasks. A facilitator, a timekeeper, a record keeper, and so on: these are familiar roles that may get rotated within classrooms and may seem important. Yet, if we consider the networks we naturally exist in—kinship networks, our online interactions with friends, the book club we may belong to—there are not always prescribed facilitators. Some people may be more vocal at shaping dynamics in a group, but they rarely own a given role like the ones given in schools.

Rather than stray away from the arbitrary-seeming roles we offer in classrooms, perhaps we should make these more exciting. Embracing the whimsy of asking groups to come together and produce via a localized and analog network, we've explored redefining the roles we might utilize in classrooms. For example, when coauthor Antero was teaching an inquiry-based project with his 9th-graders, they were tasked with ongoing exploration of local topics they had chosen. The lead-up to this work looks similar to the approaches described earlier in this chapter. As a result, by the time students were asked to work together and engage in historical analysis, the tasks they were assigned fit into familiar roles. This familiarity encouraged individual stretching into areas that might feel safely unfamiliar, and students played with the themes of critical theory that were at the heart of the unit. As an example, here are the generic roles that could be customized for the given tasks each day in class. (It is important to note that the class was in dialogue with a fictitious spider, Anansi, that allowed coauthor Antero to give playful feedback and engage in formative assessment.):

- Diplomat: helps facilitate work between group members
- Engineer: oversees construction of work
- Checkered Flag: keeps group working in a timely manner
- Tourist: looks at the work from the view of the "other"
- Portal: sends the question to Anansi via a class-specific phone number

As with the roles described above, Antero also broadened individual tasks so that half of the students in the class had unique tasks and these pairs of students could then check in with one another. The scope of group work does not have to fit into four to five student clusters. A whole class, after all, is a group. It's a community. If we take the kumbaya vibes of the well-known mantra "it takes a village" as a theoretical construct for a starting point, let us consider how this group might cull from it productive inquiry as a larger community.

Networking Beyond

Reflecting on the powerful kinship and community building they sustained, the 3D Project teachers ruminated on how this group sustained itself over time.

Christina: I think for me the one impactful thing was that who we all were was enough. So we didn't have to position ourselves as experts . . . . We could arrive with an interest, a common interest in the work of connecting our students and an urgency, the urgency that was there as well. But who we were was enough and that was true when we talked together in the hotel room [and] that was true when we were around the table.

Mary: We come from such different places and that allowed for us to listen and really hear what those different perspectives are from places around the country. So there's the community, there's the fun parts, but there's also the deep listening of what's actually different. Place really matters in this research.

We can spend a lifetime working to craft the experiences and possibilities within our classroom and not a second would be wasted. The threads for networking and collaboration are limitless even when we are counting the not-so-small handful of individuals we work with on a daily basis. Yet we also recognize that expanding these networks beyond our classroom can be incredibly productive. Christina and Mary above make interesting distinctions; the relationships fostered in the 3D Project were first brokered through online interactions. However, several face-to-face meetings solidified solidarity and friendship. Before we offer specific strategies for engaging in this work, let us first step back and illuminate the ways networking beyond our classrooms traditionally falls short.

Oftentimes, the work of networking and identifying outside an organization falls into some basic roles: either educators might be looking for an outside organization to offer an instructional or experiential service for a group (e.g., a field trip or class demonstration) or educators might be looking for temporary engagement around a topic for students (e.g., internships, beach cleanups, food drives). Such approaches can be rewarding in the short term, but we are also reminded of the words of warning from Westheimer and Kahne (2004) that these kinds of single issue–based approaches do not adequately interrogate the root causes of justice that might be tied to the issues brought up in an instructional unit.

It should be clear by now that relationships continue to be the central aspect of networks both within and beyond the walls of our classrooms. If we are able to understand shared interests—with educators at other locations, with local businesses, and with individuals across the globe—we can work toward transformational change. Rather than extractive forms of civic action in which we take materials or ideas from others, networking should encourage us to build side by side with others.

Instead of imagining networking outside of your classroom as something that primarily extends the reach and external capacities of your own civic work, we need to reorient towards an approach that inherently reframes our beliefs and embodied stances as learners. The further beyond your classroom community you might wander, the more diversity in ideas and perspectives you might encounter. This goes for both teachers and students. In our experience, we often reach out to organizations and individuals because we hope they might alter or enrich the learning possibilities for our students.

Getting Started: Critical Issue Exploration.   In our work with the 3D Project, getting students and teachers to connect beyond their local bubbles was a central factor in how the group came together. Much more than online pen pals communicating with one another, students were confronting belief systems and deeply held values that veered far away from what they would typically encounter within their neighborhoods. As a network, the students and teachers in the 3D Project were building collectively toward shared understanding. This is as important a goal in instructional work as finding mission-oriented allies. Understanding and broadening perspectives is only as possible as the links in our existing network. While you may not always be able to meet face to face with your networks, we want to call attention to the ways relationships may feel different and progress at different paces depending on the modalities on which they operate.

Of course, there are risks involved in this kind of venturing, specifically of wandering amidst an overwhelming expanse of ideas that vary in accuracy, intent, and commitment to the development of an equitable public sphere. As adults, we regularly discriminate between what is factual and what is deliberately misinformed, between the illuminative and the predatory. When we engage our young people in networking outside of our classrooms, part of our responsibility is to facilitate learning these skills. Media literacy practices need to be developed over time and encompass more than just understanding the savvy skills of what sites or ideas can be trusted or rejected. Rather, networks require deliberation and an exploration of the ideological and economic systems that they are built upon. As we noted at the beginning of the chapter, digital networks in particular are never neutral systems. They are built for consumers and producers to interact and connect while algorithmic marketing shapes pathways toward advertising and profit. This may feel miles away from the considerations you want to make in your classroom when it comes to networks; however, where else but in school will we deliberately engage young people in considering the infrastructure on which we build trust and empathy with one another?

Taking It to the Next Level: Community Walks and Asset Mapping. As we work toward common understanding and dialogue, consider who is a part of the safety net that you are weaving for yourself and your students. Who are the critical friends for the objective you are presently teaching? Can you name those individuals or groups now? Can your students? As an explicit activity, you should consider how your attempts at networking beyond your classroom are expanding the assets and skills map you hopefully began as described earlier in this chapter. This might be literal: Can you project a map of your classroom on Google Maps? Or, even better, engage in a community walk of the neighborhood around you. What are the businesses nearby? Who are the people invested in this geographic community? This kind of activity—literally getting outside of your typical teaching comfort zone—is particularly important if you teach in a place where you don't physically live yourself. Either on a digital map or on paper, start annotating the people and places nearby with which you might connect. In our digital age it might feel strange to think about the relationships that involve walking, eye contact, and pointing to shared landmarks. However, as much as we hope you'll embrace the wide variety of approaches to networking, we want to emphasize that your first steps beyond your classroom can be literal ones, going outside and seeing what the world has to offer for your learning experiences.

Once you've begun to explore the possibilities of networking across geographically local environments, you can also start looking beyond the boundaries of the walkable or commutable. Ask yourself, or have your students ask: Who else cares about the issue on which you are working? Who else might be an ally in this topic or might have students who are also interested in the issues at hand? To be clear, there are no tried-and-true approaches to reaching out to individuals. We are not giving you a script for how to contact allies. Rather, a short and direct message or phone call will be enough to determine if there is interest and capacity to explore collaboration. With students, this kind of work can feel intimidating. In our own classrooms, we would often demonstrate calling individuals by having our phones on speaker (letting the call recipient know this) and having our students listen to a professional dialogue. If students are networking with other young people, email and phone calls may make less sense than other messaging tools on social media platforms. Use the tools that are safe and naturally responsive to the contexts within which you are working.

An important consideration when looking at the limitless pathways for networking is that nothing is or should be mutually exclusive. Just as in your non-teaching social life, you interact and draw friendship and guidance from individuals online and from the people geographically around you. These are always working in concert with one another. So, absolutely, you can continue to build and explore connections locally. Who are the nonprofits, government agencies, businesses, and individuals that are synergistically committed to the same goals toward which you and your students are progressing?

You will be amazed at who will show up and help. It may not be the partner you have in mind. That activist you follow on social media or that organization that donates profits from every sale to the exact cause you are working on: they will possibly let you down with radio silence or a formulaic response. It could be great to have their support someday, but this chapter's emphasis on networking isn't about world shifting (yet): it is about shifting our own capacities and those of the students in our classrooms. What we need are a few willing participants who can work alongside us as we learn and build and dream together.

You do not need to be exhaustive in this search. Even a single partner in your work with students can prove wildly helpful. Instead of trying to find an exhaustive directory of everyone working on your chosen issues, you only need to find one critical friend. Remember these are the stakes of movement building and civic transformation in our classrooms: a network of even one more person thrives when it is a network that flourishes on relationships and shared interests. Recall the asset-mapping activity with your students; you are implicitly engaging in this work of identifying shared interests and beliefs every time you reach out to others. These are complex literacy skills that are inferred and usually not actively taught to students or to teachers.

As you continue to innovate networking practices beyond the walls of your classroom, remember the common goal: We are not extracting expertise just to bring it back into our classroom. We are building. We are building dialogue, empathy, and solidarity over time. The civic possibilities of networking must work toward innovative networks of shared interests and social desires.

Networking Toward Freedom

The presentation schedule for the members of the Council of Youth Research was a full one in the coming weeks. In addition to academic conferences, students would be sharing their work at the local UCLA Labor Center in downtown Los Angeles, tailoring their work to school site–specific presentations, and uploading their work to share via digital resources. The current moment was filled with data analysis, preparation, and building out a list of actionable steps to be ready for these different events, as well as the possibilities for media coverage and the day-to-day work of staying on top of actual classwork. The activities of this youth participatory action research collective demonstrated how much work needed to be done to disrupt long-standing educational inequities.

In pursuing their contemporary, research-backed calls for educational change, the students found themselves in the curious space of conversing with and working alongside some academic ancestors. The team from Locke High School, for example, didn't simply explore the role of food deserts and the lack of healthy options around their school community in Watts; they also forged linguistic, ideological, and activist connections with the work of 19th-century Italian philosopher Antonio Gramsci. This seemingly odd connection was made as students played with multiple meanings of the word "organic." It started with food. In order to demonstrate the different options that existed in their neighborhood compared to wealthier communities nearby, the students used Google Maps to illustrate the simple point that the nearest organic grocery store—a Trader Joe's or a Whole Foods, for example—was many miles away from their school. In effect, if the students wanted anything organic, it would have to originate from them. This exploration of organic food sparked an association for them with a Gramsci article that we had introduced to them about organic intellectuals—leaders who grew from communities without the need for formal titles. The students loved the word play and conceptual connection.

Describing the role of "organic intellectuals" as engaging in work that will intentionally "change and influence culture, morality and political agendas," these students saw a clear parallel between their work today and that of an Italian Marxist best known for his journals maintained while in prison. On seeing the students' final presentation, "This Ain't Trader Joes—The Real Organic: Growing Organic Leaders from Concrete," it became clear that these students were not simply building on the ideas of Gramsci (or Tupac Shakur, as their presentation title references his book's title, *The Rose that Grew from Concrete*). Rather, these were students working alongside individuals from the past in an effort to transform the present. This speculative act of

networking was one that spanned space, time, and the assumptions that the dead only haunt the imaginations of the present.

There's a big problem with the majority of networking practices and
tools—including those discussed in this chapter thus far. The problem
is one of presentism. Networks assume everyone is working at the same
time and scale as one another. We might learn from our ancestors,
and we might plan for future generations, but our models of networking do not presume that these are groups with which we are engaged
in working today. This is a huge loss. As we seek civic innovation for
brighter possible futures, we need to be working in solidarity across the
boundaries of time. We are not speaking to some sort of time travel or
fanciful visions of science fiction. Instead, we want to engage in two
forms of interrogation.

First, we must interrogate the beliefs and ideas that have been
fomented by past civic actors: What are the efforts around sustainabil-
ity or social justice or freedom that we can adapt and build upon, for
instance? Second, what strategies did these past groups and individuals enact? We tend to imagine new technologies driving social change
today. However, as our exploration of digital tools makes clear, these
tools can often hamper and blind us to how civic action and discourse
unfolds. The conversations on a platform like Twitter or Instagram
are limited to the modalities that exist there; they may offer multimodal forms of communication, but they cannot recreate the gestures,
cadence, and physical presence of in-person dialogue. Invoking the title
of Tom Standage's (1998) book *The Victorian Internet,* the practices of
social networking existed long before digital technologies tethered us
to flashing screens. Instead, we must recall the truly wireless societies
that thrived before the world wide web and how solidarity can cross
time and space.

Getting Started: Expanding Networks Into the Not-Yet. Networking across temporalities requires us to update past perspectives
and carry them into contemporary contexts. The aforementioned freedom schools that thrived in the heyday of the civil rights movement,
for example, offer clear strategies for how to invoke informal schooling

approaches today. In our work with the Council of Youth Research, we considered the spirit of this past movement, but frankly did not fully lift up and extend this model. This is the iterative step—an imaginative one—that networking toward freedom must include.

Taking It to the Next Level: Playful Networking Opportunities. As we'll explore in the next chapter's focus on imagination, we also believe there are ways we can build intentional pathways toward measurable action through leveling up ideas grounded in fiction. The made-up stories we tell of alternate ways of being or of future pathways can help transform the real world. It may seem silly, but building networks that stem from fiction and from whimsy can be powerful. We are reminded of the rise of the Harry Potter Alliance (HPA) in the mid-2000s, for example. Although this was a network of fans existing in the present real world, the group's participants carried forward the values represented within the fantasy novel series in order to engage in different forms of civic action.

The Work of the Network

Like wiring or pipes in a home, a network is only as strong as the links that are made. One faulty connection and you are left in the dark or in a mess. We say this not to caution you to look warily at the students in your classroom. Instead, we want to recognize two key factors when it comes to developing the networks you will sustain with your students and—for longer stretches of time—with your colleagues. First, networks require ongoing maintenance and work. While we all have some friends or family members who can fall out of touch for prolonged periods of time and still snap back to close and loving familiarity, most relationships require continuous check-ins and care. This is the work of the network. Second, we cannot take these links and the assumed values within them for granted. Determining if all members of a network share the same perspectives about an issue, are working toward shared goals, or have similar theories of change is important. It's less important that you attain total agreement amongst members of a network; healthy dialogue has always been at the center of thriving democracies.

Rather, getting to a place of knowing what individuals believe is imperative. So is knowing that our beliefs change, particularly within complex learning environments like our classrooms. As we focused on the what and the how of civic networking in this chapter, we offer these closing words to remind you to stay vigilant to the changes and inactivity of the nodes of your network. In the next chapter, we will work together to imagine the new worlds that these networks can eventually bring into being.

Discussion Questions

1. How are you developing a system for you and your students to understand their interests, expertise, and shared goals? What kinds of approaches might allow you to map or graph these connections?
2. Which local individuals or organizations would help you with your pedagogical vision? What presently is stopping you from connecting with them?
3. How are your civic goals tied to historic movements or ideas? How can you carry forward and update the practices and strategies utilized in previous eras and contexts?
4. What are your strategies for staying up to date on the feelings and ideas that are felt by the myriad members of your network?

Chapter 6

||||||||||||||||||

Building the Future Through Civic Imagination

You have likely heard some variation of the well-known biblical proverb, "There is nothing new under the sun." It is often cited to highlight the cyclical nature of human discovery and remind us that what we may consider novel often has historical precedent. However, in an unpublished poem, science fiction writer Octavia Butler invokes the proverb only to turn it on its head by adding the addendum: "but there are new suns" (as quoted in Benjamin, 2017). Butler's words jolt us out of the complacency that can settle in our minds as we traverse educational and civic landscapes year after year that appear impervious to change. As the school years and election cycles progress, what were once innovative practices imperceptibly calcify into just the way things are done. That is, until we experience a moment—often sparked by encounters with art or play—that renders the familiar strange and offers the tantalizing potential of alternative possibilities, new worlds. We begin to ask, "What if?" What if schooling as we know it ceased to exist; what forms of teaching and learning could we build? What if democracy as we know it disappeared; what other systems could we devise for governing ourselves?

These practices of imagination are not often considered the domain of civic education, or really of most of the subjects taught in school today. Why spend time dreaming about what doesn't exist when there is so much to learn about how this world currently works? Indeed, it can seem like a luxury or privilege to play and imagine different realities amid the sobering challenges facing society today. It can seem more logical to spend time learning how current levers of power work—how a bill becomes a law, say—and how to incrementally improve the social structures that govern our daily lives than to muse about radical change.

Yet this logic only holds if we associate imagination with pure fantasy and view it as a means of escape or distraction from the world as it is. This is not the perspective that we—or the speculative fiction writers and social game designers we will discuss in this chapter—take. Instead, we conceptualize the imagination as a deeply visionary and constructive capacity of the human mind, one that engages with rather than retreats from our existing society but refuses to concede to its inevitability or perpetual continuation. The cultivation of civic imagination involves an insistence upon dreaming alongside youth of what might be in order to stimulate creativity, joy, and change.

As we discussed in the previous storytelling and networking chapters, tethering ourselves too tightly to the civic institutions and ideas of today runs the risk of stifling the energy and originality needed to build new worlds capable of managing the unprecedented challenges that will confront our students in the future. In this chapter, we advocate for the crucial role of play, dreams, and imagination in our pedagogy and explore ways to infuse our practice with this world-building commitment. We begin with an exploration of the roles played by art and games in supporting social change and then interrogate the reasons behind the conspicuous absence of dreaming and play in many classrooms today. We then return to stories drawn from the communities we have been getting to know throughout this book to elucidate opportunities and resources for injecting more civic hope, magic, and fun into your practice with your students.

Our journey will illustrate how we can imagine new relationships, civic pathways, and visionary futures through the design of our instruction (see Table 6.1).

Table 6.1 Interrogating and Innovating with Imagination

IMAGINATION LENS	WHAT TO INTERROGATE	TOOLS TO INNOVATE
Civic Pathways	1. How can we apply our knowledge of current social challenges and existing mechanisms of civic engagement to the practice of "gamifying"/playing with new approaches to problem-solving?	Gamifying the Curriculum
"Magic" Solutions	1. What "magic" solutions could we develop to solve our society's most intractable challenges? 2. How can we translate our wild civic imagining into efforts to transform the world that currently exists?	Exercising Our Magical Thinking Capacity Civic "Deus ex Machina" Experiment
Visionary Futures	1. How can imaginatively disrupting the taken-for-granted values and institutions in our lives spur creative visions of possible civic futures?	World-Building

The Importance of Civic Imagination: Classroom and Community Contexts

We began this chapter with the words of visionary fiction writer Octavia Butler. In the summer of 2020, as the United States reeled from the COVID-19 pandemic, uprisings against racial injustice, and the ongoing effects of climate change and political unrest, Butler's novel, *The Parable of the Sower*, reappeared on bestseller lists 27 years after its initial publication date. This story of a Black teenager navigating a postapocalyptic California in the year 2025 resonated anew with many who were shocked by the prescience of Butler's imagination and compelled to contemplate potential visions, both hopeful and catastrophic, for the future of society.

Educators have long understood the power of art to both spark reflection about universal human experiences and offer insights into specific social issues, time periods, and communities; hence the inclusion of literature and art courses throughout the curriculum. While art can sometimes offer escape from social realities, it more often than not offers intense engagement with the world around us—even when taking place in fantasy settings. Its unique role in civic life stems from its ostensibly fictive or unreal form. Because art is free from the requirement to remain faithful at all times to factually accurate depictions of the real world, it offers a canvas upon which the mind can roam and experiment with alternative possibilities of how we might organize society or address common challenges.

This creative thinking can then be applied back to our current reality in order to push past the status quo, spurring new perspectives about long-standing assumptions and suggesting new approaches to enduring challenges. Yet such application of art to democratic world building requires careful cultivation on the part of educators. Art educator and scholar Maxine Greene (2000) encourages teachers to reject the binary that is often erected in schools between art and civic learning. Instead of conceptualizing art as nonacademic and fun while situating civics as academic and serious, she calls for pedagogies that take a both/and approach. Greene argues that discussions about and creation of art in school supports the development of students' "social imagination," which she defines as "the capacity to invent visions of what should be and what might be in our deficient society, on the streets where we live, in our schools" (p. 5). Considerations of what the future "should" or "might" be must engage with values, which provides the opening for us educators to connect the social imagination and art to dreams of equitable and just futures.

Social imagination is cultivated not only through art but through play as well. What is play but the creation of something new out of the filaments of thought, collaboration, and curiosity? Although the media often portrays gamers as aloof and cordoned off in front of screens, sequestered by themselves, the contexts for digital and tabletop play are largely collaborative and social (Chen, 2011; Nardi, 2010; Pearce & Artemesia, 2009). As coauthor Antero has written about previously, when people play games they often do so with other people and in contexts that forge powerful relationships both within a game and beyond it (Garcia, 2019). Engaging in a tabletop role-playing game like *Dungeons & Dragons* is an act of collective writing, dreaming, and building. As a group, players negotiate and arbitrate the systems of how a world is created and explored. This is speculative and civic work that is manifested as play. Board games also—from Monopoly to Settlers of Catan to Twister—are acts of group collaboration, even if the worlds they inhabit are abstract or defined by the logics of capitalism and competition.

The constraints of noninteractive video games confine players to the worlds and actions programmed by the games' designers. However, even within a closed system like *Grand Theft Auto*, the potential for creative and speculative creation always exists; as Cortez et al. (2022) illuminates, these are games that can be bent toward liberatory forms of dreaming and play.

The concept of the social imagination serves as a reminder that we need to be able to imagine change—in ourselves, in others, and in society—before we can enact it. If we do not exercise our social imaginations and capacities for play, we may well preemptively reject novel approaches to public challenges as outlandish, or fail to even think of them in the first place, rather than seeing them as the seeds of social transformation. Artists and game designers who create within the genre of visionary or speculative expression invite those who engage with their work to imagine future worlds in which the forms of oppression and inequity that mar our present are disrupted or even nonexistent, with the conscious intention of inspiring critique and social movements in the here and now—first in the mind and then on the ground. Walidah Imarisha (2015), visionary fiction writer and activist, reminds us that many campaigns for justice and civil rights were once considered outlandish or impossible to achieve—until they weren't. As she puts it, "All organizing is science fiction" (p. x).

Imarisha integrates fiction writing and world building into

workshops that she leads for educators and community organizers to help catalyze the creative thinking necessary to dream beyond the bounds of incremental reform toward fundamental social metamorphosis. This approach is being taken up across multiple fields; as introduced in Chapter 2, Jenkins and colleagues (2020) utilize a framework of civic imagination to analyze the role of art and popular culture in opening the hearts and minds of the public to social change. And, as we have repeated throughout these chapters, we are committed to bringing this spirit of civic imagination to public schooling to transform teaching and learning with young people through the framework of speculative civic literacies. Instead of simply preparing young people for the world as it is, which has continually demonstrated its shortcomings in addressing the most pressing challenges, we educators have the ethical responsibility to offer them the resources and guidance needed to build the world to come. Unfortunately, schools are not currently structured to support such a vision—a situation we tackle next.

Interrogating the Barriers to Imagination in Schools

The rationale underlying the dearth of imaginative expression in schools is a bit of a paradox; it is treated as simultaneously too inconsequential and too powerful to be cultivated in the classroom. On the one hand, as discussed earlier, imagination as expressed through the creation of art or through game play is considered frivolity in the face of the mountains of content that must be evaluated through high-stakes testing to prepare students for college, career, and civic life. On the other hand, imagination as expressed through engagement with books and histories that explore topics like race, gender, and sexuality from nondominant and critical perspectives is often considered such a powerful and potentially dangerous influence upon the opinions of young people that it must be controlled through actions like book bans or curriculum audits.

The uneasy relationship between schooling and imagination is a manifestation of the clash between multiple purposes of public education. When education is considered a utilitarian commodity that translates into benefits in the academic and economic marketplace, such as earning college admission or getting a job, its focus turns toward concrete bodies of knowledge and skills that correspond to those goals. We regularly hear our elementary school colleagues bemoan the encroachment of "serious" academic learning into the earliest grade levels, which increasingly pushes out opportunities for art and other creative electives in favor of tested subjects of literacy and math. This practice reinforces the perspective that imagination is not core to learning but is an add-on that can be shifted to after-school or home settings.

Yet even as this dismissive treatment of imagination continues, the proliferation of efforts across the country to prevent students from exposure to perspectives in art and literature that contradict or simply differ from those held by family or community members indicates that imagination is still a formidable force for expansive learning. The ideas students encounter in school matter not just in utilitarian ways but also for more expansive purposes of social dreaming. Consider the efforts in states across the country to prevent students from reading texts by authors of color that critique American exceptionalism and reveal the persistent presence of racism in U.S. society. Or those that seek to ban discussions of LGBTQ+ identities. These efforts do not simply indicate the unwillingness of some to respect identities and ideas beyond their own, or even simply doubt in the ability of youth to develop their own opinions. They also suggest that the architects of such efforts are so afraid of what might happen if children have their horizons expanded (e.g., developing respect for others, finding common ground) that such horizons should be closed off in schools.

In effect, these efforts prove just how transformative the cultivation of imagination can be, as well as the role that public schools can play in fostering equitable democratic communities. Imagining experiences outside of our individual frames of reference has the potential to foster the critical civic empathy we have discussed in previous chapters. Such empathy is the first step in the creation of movements toward solidarity and common cause in the face of shared civic challenges. Public schools are sites where the cultivation of critical civic empathy can occur through the intentional development of opportunities to play and dream wildly. This is not a way to avoid college and career and the very real world our students are entering, but a rigorous and creative way to imagine the worlds they deserve and then take stock of what must begin changing in the here and now to get there.

Innovating Our Commitment to Imagination: Moving From Theory to Practice

Integrating civic imagination into our courses can take countless forms depending on the nature of the inquiry your students develop, the journey that collective storytelling takes your classes on, and the ideas that emerge from your developing community networks. The key is to continually remind yourself that challenging social inequity and experiencing joy are not mutually exclusive activities. While we have repeatedly referenced the gravity of the social challenges facing our students, we also recognize the very real threats of burnout and empathy fatigue that can occur if we do not tap into the human need for finding laughter and silliness and play in the course of civic learning.

Each of our focus learning communities cultivated imagination in different ways. In the Black Cloud game, students role-played as various civic actors and dreamed up fictional solutions to a very real community challenge, thereby imagining new civic pathways that could influence their future actions in real life. When students in the 3D Project were encouraged to dream of a civic future free of intractable social problems, they experimented with magic solutions as a conduit to discussing existing levers of change. When the MS 50 debate team engaged in tournaments discussing immigration, they tried to get judges and their peers to join them in imagining visionary futures free of borders as a first step to challenging xenophobia today.

Imagining Civic Pathways

Sometimes civic pathways are crafted through happenstance and play. In the midst of the Black Cloud game, students would often improvise narrative elements that led the game designers (coauthor Antero and a team of artists led by UC Berkeley professor Greg Niemeyer) to reconfigure the game based on the ideas of young people. These unexpected moments—a student questioning the placement of an air quality sensor in a dry-cleaning facility or asking if the Black Cloud was a good dancer—sometimes felt silly. However, as an instructional and design team, the adults took student ideas as guidance for how this open-ended story might conclude. By the time the game wrapped in the final weeks of August, students found themselves in a local art gallery witnessing a costumed Black Cloud dance its way onto a public bus and politely excuse itself from the city; their efforts pushed the pollution and threat of the Black Cloud out of their communities.

These civic pathways were traced in student writing as well. Early on, the Black Cloud would send clues to aspects of the game communicating in "leet speak"—early internet language that utilized numbers as letters (e.g., "l33t sp3ak"). Mimicking the Black Cloud's speech pattern, several of the students participating in the Black Cloud picked up the fictional premise of the game and added to it. Rather than a game or curriculum happening to them, these students remediated the events of the world around them as part of the fictional setting of a sentient cloud hovering over the skies of Los Angeles. For example, several weeks into the gaming activity, an earthquake shook the school, causing a safety evacuation:

"! th33nk da 3arthquak3 had sumt!in 2 do w!t da dr33m ! had bout da blac cloud & da m3ssag3 !t wuz tryin 2 giv3 m3" [I think the earthquake had something to do with the dream I had about the Black Cloud and the message it was trying to give me.]

Invoking the real world change around him, Esteban took a dream he shared—of the Black Cloud communicating with him—and connected it to the earthquake. While we talk elsewhere about the data and advocacy that stemmed from this activity, we highlight here the Black Cloud's playful elements—the ways students were encouraged to add to the storytelling aspects of the game and step into an alternate version of their city in which clouds talk and earthquakes are tied to Twitter communication.

At first blush, these creative posts might not seem to embody the same kinds of transformative change as the policy demands the students issued or their use of data for understanding the world around them. However, we want to emphasize the civic acts of interpreting real world phenomena through imaginative storytelling. What new interpretations of the world are possible when we layer our imagination on top of the taken for granted?

Getting Started: Gamifying the Curriculum. It may not seem easy to create an entire alternate reality game and have your students communicate with fictitious characters. Admittedly, coauthor Antero was able to collaborate with a team of UC Berkeley artists through a grant the team received. However, we want to emphasize that the basic elements of play are embedded in how children interact and dream. Schools create contexts where students are not expected to utilize their imagination in the ways that Esteban takes up. Rather than trying to create complex games, seek out pockets of playful areas for students to ask "what if?" or to pose hypotheticals: Why might the ground have quaked on this auspicious August afternoon? Why must the reading assessments determine what kinds of literature students are allowed to check out in the school library? These questions may not seem like games, but they can become playful and speculative. In our experience, creating playful experiences requires trying to prod at the perceived boundaries of schools. What is determined permissible or transgressive? How might you let your students see you as silly in order to see themselves stepping out of the comfort zone of traditional schooling?

Taking it to the Next Level: Turning Games into Transformational Civic Events. Imbuing your classroom with practices of play is only the beginning. By organizing classroom activities around curiosity, we open up possibilities for students to naturally take on more active roles as civic innovators within our classrooms and beyond. For example, sustaining a classroom that pushes on the boundaries of school may not seem natural or easy. The kinds of spaces where kids can regularly ask why, playfully nudge the environment into more imaginative directions, and offer new kinds of solutions to the day-to-day rigamarole of schooling are spaces that dismantle the traditional power dynamics of classrooms. In this way, play—from our civic framing here—intentionally ruptures adult-centered authority and seeks to level the playing field within classrooms.

What if society writ-large were to do the same?

It is not that gaming must be invoked systematically for every individual but that playful agents—ourselves and our students—can view the world through a lens that asks "why" and "what if?" Constantly pushing for these questions is about naturalizing the process of questioning and transforming the world around us.

Imagining Magic Solutions

As students wrapped up their cross-school civic issue dialogues in the final months of the school year, the 3D Project teachers felt inspired by the demonstrations of empathy and curiosity that they witnessed. Many of the connections felt refreshing and hopeful compared with the rancorous examples of political discourse they saw broadcast each day across media outlets. The musings of the adults turned toward the future. Could this energy be sustained? What did the next generation hope to experience as they grew further into their civic identities? The teachers decided to go to the source and ask the students themselves.

The third design cycle of the 3D Project asked a simple but provocative question: What kind of civic future do you see? Teachers encouraged students to take this question in any direction they chose (Is the future a comedy? A tragedy? A triumph?) and gave them freedom to develop any type of artifact they liked to express their responses. Some students took a pragmatic approach; a group in Alaska developed a PowerPoint presentation about their "vision of a 2050 conservative America" while a group in Pennsylvania crafted signs that they imagined would still be needed at protests in the years to come: "End Police Brutality." "Black Lives Matter."

Yet some students in Michigan and Texas, influenced by the comic book–inspired film *Black Panther*, began dreaming about civic superheroes who could magically solve what they saw as the most stubborn and troubling social problems in their communities. Kelly from Texas created "The Lifesaver," whose superpower is "to reduce the temperature of the Earth" to fight global warming. Andy, her classmate, created "Nourish" who can "turn any object into food" in order to feed the hungry. Simone, a student from Michigan, created an entire backstory for her superhero:

> *Home Girl has the power to create homes and take families off of the streets (also people who are on the verge of getting put out). She got her power to create homes for the homeless by once being homeless herself. She slept in abandoned buses and homes. One night after sleeping in an abandoned bus she woke up in the middle of the night. She saw a bright green object glowing. Home Girl got up and walked towards it. She picked up the glowing ball of who knows what. It exploded all over her! The next morning she woke—but she woke up in a nice home. How weird was that, she wondered. Home Girl knew she had something special.*
>
> *One day Home Girl was driving under a popular bridge called the H Town Bridge. There were multiple homeless people. Men, women, and even children. So she went to talk to them all. She gathered them up and told them to close their eyes. Home Girl then transported them to an open field. She explained that homes would be built for them and they would not have to worry about a thing. They were full of joy! Home Girl then created their homes for them. Everyone was amaz[ed]—but more than anything, grateful. Home Girl was able to take multiple families off of the streets. Home Girl also provides utilities for each home she builds so that people don't have to be worried about anything but finding work and bettering themselves.*

Simone's teacher, Peter, wondered if these superheroes could be read as expressions of despair—the last imaginative resort of young people who have seen the adults around them fail to address suffering. Janelle, the Texas teacher, heard this concern but also suggested to her students that "dreaming of magical solutions first might help us think more creatively in the here and now."

The 3D Project superhero activity illustrates both the insufficiency of the binary separating procedural and creative thinking in civic learning and the enduring nervousness that we teachers continue to feel about engaging in serious play in the classroom. Through the creation of Home Girl, Simone demonstrated several elements of real world civic engagement: (1) she identified a problem in her community, including specific places where the problem is most evident; (2) she identified a (magical) solution that speaks to the real need for both housing and support with monthly utility expenses; and (3) she recognized that those who experience challenges themselves (e.g., Home Girl's previous experience of homelessness) are often well positioned to address them. These are skills that are eminently transferable to existing social institutions.

Yet Peter was still nervous about whether engaging in this activity in class could be construed as a retraction or distraction from civic learning. Such hesitancy reminds us of how powerful the turn away from imagination can be in our schools and the intention that we need to bring to our planning if we hope to recapture this spirit of experimentation in our pedagogy. As Janelle reassured Peter, magical thinking can indeed be a powerful exercise to dream new futures and begin to build those dreams in the here and now. Let's consider how to take the first steps.

Getting Started: Exercising Our Magical Thinking Capacity. Imagination is not something that we need to plan separate or additional opportunities for within our classes; indeed, such planning would only reinforce the aforementioned binary between so-called serious academic work and silly play. We can instead integrate the practice of imagination into our curriculum by centering its role within our discussions of civic transformation. As the earlier Imarisha quote reminds us, social change can appear fantastical until it actually occurs. Encouraging young people to exercise their capacity for magical thinking will prepare them for the creative and outside-the-box thinking that is often needed to disrupt entrenched structures of inequity.

Magical thinking can live alongside the other world-building commitments that we have already discussed in previous chapters, beginning with inquiry. The very act of identifying a civic challenge can itself be a step toward imagination if we as teachers nurture social dreaming; after all, students are already wondering why a particular situation exists and whether it might be improved. We simply have to resist the way we have been socialized by traditional approaches to civic learning to immediately think within the confines of incrementalism.

Let's take Simone's choice of homelessness as an example of an inquiry topic. The traditional approach would immediately direct Simone toward detailing the circumstances causing individuals to become unhoused and the potential policies and institutions that could contribute to ameliorating this problem. The magical thinking approach suggests that before we narrow our vision to the pragmatic, we tease out the utopian vision of society; instead of following up the question of "why" with "how" to act within the confines of what exists, we encourage students to ask "why can't" and "what if." Why can't everyone be given a safe and comfortable home for free? What if everyone didn't have to worry about utilities or rent? What could they dedicate their energies toward?

While these might seem like pie-in-the-sky questions, taking them seriously and allowing students to explore their implications offers them the opportunity to clarify the values they hold dear and consider the extent to which those values are reflected in current societal structures. Questioning why housing cannot be a basic human right in our country leads to fascinating existential questions about labor, personal responsibility, and capitalism itself. It also leads to countless complex follow-up questions about how the logistics of free housing could even work. These questions can be explored through storytelling, another of our world-building commitments. Students could dream up various scenarios informed by their experiences and beliefs, constrained only by the limits of their imaginations. What if money didn't exist? What if citizens participated in mutual aid to get what they needed?

Naturally, students will prioritize different values and conceptualize utopian solutions according to frameworks that spring from their own experience. As we discussed in the networking chapter, we sometimes have a hard time stepping outside the boundaries of what we know when conceptualizing civic futures individually, particularly if we do not often interact with those from whom we differ. This limitation applies to play and dreaming as well, which is why being in open and vulnerable conversation with others is crucial to expanding our capacity for magical thinking. Whether with other students or adults in the community, conversation partners can help us stretch our imaginations by offering new possibilities or challenging our ideas.

Again, this dreaming need not stand in opposition to more practical considerations. Rather, it serves to deepen students' understanding of the roots of civic decision making and envision alternatives, even those that are not yet possible, before delving into the realities of working with what currently exists.

Taking It to the Next Level: Civic Deus ex Machina Experiment.

Make no mistake about it: Magical thinking is difficult. While you may assume that students will take to it quickly and seamlessly, it is important to keep in mind the power of the socialization that we all experience as we move through K–12 schooling that makes it harder and harder to dream big. As a result, we need to give students time to experiment on a small scale with imagination. Once students have increased their capacity for social dreaming, they may be ready to develop the entire backstory of a civic superhero, for instance. Creating narrative worlds governed by magical thinking requires a level of detail and internal logic that demonstrates sophisticated critical thinking about how civic life, both real and imagined, does and could work.

The 3D Project superhero activity is just one example of what writers and readers know as a "deus ex machina" literally translated from Latin as "god from the machine." It is a literary device in which a person, object, or plot twist is introduced from nowhere into a seemingly irresolvable situation in order to provide a happy ending. For example, think of Dorothy simply waking up to realize "it was all a dream" in *The Wizard of Oz* or Home Girl getting the power to build homes from a "glowing ball." Even though it is often characterized as a lazy device to wrap up realistic narrative fiction, it can become a gateway to elaborate creativity when the need to be realistic is taken away. To take this activity to the next level, you could have students detail the levers that create magic solutions to problems and draw comparisons to the levers of change that currently exist to address those same challenges and the circumstances that stand in the way of them functioning.

Imagining Visionary Futures

¿Por qué? ¿Por qué no podemos imaginar una nación y un debate sin bordes?

[Why? Why can't we imagine a nation and a debate without borders?]

After the MS 50 students opened each debate round with their poetry, this is the question they posed to the judge and the opposing team. While they read these words, they distributed fully translated copies of their speeches to everyone in the room. When they qualified for national tournaments, Principal Honoroff supplemented these handouts with the offer of live translation services in each round. As he explained, "I really didn't know if this would even be allowed or if judges would just disqualify us, but I thought it was an important stance to take." The translation was not being offered simply to ensure clear and open communication across lines of linguistic difference; it also represented a physical enactment of the visionary future that students sought to make with their case—a world without linguistic or geographic borders.

Before they could share this vision with others, the debaters had to internalize it themselves. They spent their after-school practices trying to imagine a borderless society. One student, Shawn, was skeptical: "If we got rid of borders, people would just fight all the time." Another student, Ofelia, suggested, "We would have to accept our differences." Ms. Mariana, one of their coaches, reminded them how seamlessly they weaved variations of both English and Spanish into their speech depending on what they wanted to express as a way to explain deconstructing binaries. "And this is why our case is different," she explained. "We are the only ones calling for the value of all humans and the abolishing of borders through bilingual pedagogy."

Nuestra vernácula se infiltra en el espacio de debate y resiste el silenciamiento que ocurre dentro del status quo. ¡Ya no permitiremos que nuestro discurso sea excluido dentro de este espacio!

[Our vernacular infiltrates the debate space and resists the silencing that occurs within the status quo. We will no longer allow our discourse to be excluded within this space!]

The debaters knew that judges might not grasp or appreciate the philosophical argument they were making; indeed, they lost several rounds when judges deemed their case off-topic. But this was not how the debaters chose to measure their success. They instead saw each match as an opportunity to disrupt the worldviews of peers and teachers within the debate community and enlist them—if just for 60 minutes—in rigorous deliberation and dreaming about alternative ways of living.

Our affirmation of a no-border politic ruptures the status quo de jure discrimination created by the labels of "legal" and "illegal," which both the resolution and the border are based on. Our affirmation is the ultimate reduction of restrictions on immigration; it is the removal of the "legal" and "illegal" immigrant categories.

By inviting their judges and opponents to envision a future in which national borders—and in turn dominant conceptualizations of immigration—are eliminated, the MS 50 debate team disrupted not only the traditional format of debate but also the nature and purpose of civic learning itself. Their act of imagination represented a refusal to be bound by the social arrangements in which we currently find ourselves and a reminder that alternative universes are possible. It is an extension of the 3D Project superhero thought experiment; once students can dream about magically eliminating homelessness, they can dream up an entire world in which individuals completely reimagine the very nature of housing and living in community.

Again, the purpose of this imaginative world building is not to escape reality or dream for the sake of dreaming, although these activities also have a place in learning. Rather, it is to develop habits of mind in which young people can decenter the taken-for-granted assumptions of civic life and, by making the familiar strange, remind themselves that structures and institutions that humans have created can be changed when they no longer serve collective aims of equity and justice. As the MS 50 students show us, such imagination is pedagogical; each time they presented their case to another debate team, they created cognitive dissonance that could spark dialogue and new ways of thinking about the foundational values and practices upon which we build our shared societies. We have the opportunity to support such critical and creative thinking in our teaching as well.

Getting Started: World Building. Earlier in this chapter we introduced you to the ideas of visionary fiction writer Walidah Imarisha, who draws metaphorical parallels between community organizing and science fiction because of their common basis in imagining utopian possibilities. Along with fellow activist, adrienne maree brown, Imarisha edited *Octavia's Brood* (2015), a book in which individuals involved in social movement work wrote short stories describing what a future that fully embodied the fruits of their efforts could look like. Imarisha notes in the introduction that many of these people had never written fiction before and were nervous about attempting such a practice, but through collaboration and dialogue they were able to take what they knew from their own experience and express it creatively. She describes telling them, "We are dreaming new worlds every time we think about the changes we want to make in the world" (p. 4). Upon reflection, she realized, "[They] just needed a little space, and perhaps permission to immerse themselves fully in their visionary selves" (p. 4).

We see great potential in applying this process to our work with students in the classroom who also need space and permission to dream of worlds worthy of them. In previous chapters we discussed how the knowledge bases in each of our academic disciplines are grounded in particular assumptions or ways of viewing the world—and how asking questions or engaging in storytelling around those assumptions can serve as a portal into innovative learning. An extension of this work is to invite students to imagine worlds in which those assumptions are disrupted or absent altogether. The laws of human behavior, the norms of statistical modeling, economic theories. What would worlds look like in which these could be bent or reimagined in ways that address issues that matter to students and promote more harmonious and compassionate relations? Storytelling structures can be applied to explicating these worlds, from setting and characters to plot and imagery.

Another resource that teachers can draw from is *Practicing Futures*, a handbook written by artists and scholars Gabriel Peters-Lazaro and Sangita Shresthova (2020). This text offers a series of workshop-facilitation ideas drawn from their work with community organizations that utilize popular culture and art to activate participants' civic imagination. Complete with agendas, icebreakers, guiding questions, timing, and examples, the workshops can give students structured support to imagine worlds and build action plans that translate their dreams into advocacy in today's world for social change. These can be modified to address the needs of particular groups of students, community contexts, and academic needs.

Returning to the possibilities of play and world building, we offer some key advice. We know this can feel overwhelming. First, start small. Taking the two-word phrase, "what if," invite your students to question what if the inequities around them were otherwise. What if we could imagine the cafeteria food as better, the tardy policies abolished, the abandoned housing structure across the street repurposed? These simple acts of world building may seem like idle dreaming, but even in questioning—what Freire (1970) called "problem posing"—we can see students crafting playful new civic pathways from the small act of questioning. Second, as these examples and the Black Cloud demonstrate, emphasize world building tied to the familiar. If there is an earthquake or similar local issue shaping student life, how might that invoke playful opportunities for imagination and design?

Taking It to the Next Level: Extending Collaboration. While many of the debate teams that MS 50 students encountered at tournaments were so surprised by the team's case and focused on winning that they sought to simply argue against or dismiss the invitation to imagine a borderless world, some were intrigued enough to play—even if just for the duration of the round—with this alternative reality and dream about how people might coexist if national boundaries ceased to exist. The only thing more powerful than individual imagination is collective imagination; witnessing young people take seriously the dreams of others and seek to contribute to the construction of fantastic new realities seems to us to be the foundation for hopeful civic transformation.

As with the other commitments in this book, the practice of imagination can be meaningfully expanded when the invitation to participate reaches beyond individual classrooms. Just as every individual brings unique experiences, voice, values, and capacities to civic life, so too do they bring unique dreams. The opportunity to see what another person's imagined utopia might look like and put it into conversation with one's own will undoubtedly expose differences that can raise questions that might not otherwise have been asked and spark dialogues that might not otherwise have occurred.

Acting as If

"You have to act as if it were possible to radically transform the world. And you have to do it all the time."
—Angela Davis (as quoted in Anderson, 2014)

Each time we read this quote from Angela Davis, we linger on the choice of the words "as if." Those words feel a bit unsettling at first. Do they imply that transformation is indeed possible all the time—or that fundamental social change is a dream always a bit out of reach that we must keep pursuing anyway? Each time, we realize that the genius of the quote is that both readings are appropriate. We need to think and speak and act in collaboration with others with the understanding that the world can change in momentous ways even when such change comes too slowly or stalls or even retreats; it is through such constant imagination and hope that it eventually does. The advances that have been made toward honoring the full humanity of minoritized communities in this country, though far from sufficient, might have seemed unimaginable to some not too long ago. It was through the persistent work of those who could imagine a better future that a better future was brought into being. Hope is a discipline and one that we must instill in our young people through the joy of imagination as they continue the struggle toward more equitable civic futures.

Discussion Questions

1. Do students have the opportunity to play and dream when they are in your classroom? When they are at school? Consider when and where these opportunities arise and any barriers to imagination that may exist.

2. Engage in some imagining yourself. If you could radically transform your classroom—the way it looks, what happens in it, how teaching and learning occurs—what is your ideal vision? What do your imaginings tell you about the civic values and relationships that you hope to cultivate with your students?

3. What opportunities exist in your content area for students to play with assumptions about how the world works and engage in alternative world building?

4. How could you cultivate imagination as a habit of mind with your students as a regular practice?

Chapter 7

||||||||||||||||||||

Building the Future Through Civic Advocacy

A dvocacy may seem at first blush like something ancillary to the central goals of learning in schools. Sure, it seems civics-y, but does it merit an entire chapter in this book? Many of the ways advocating as an action and advocacy as a stance are taken up in formal education practices can seem tokenizing or blandly symbolic. This chapter seeks to rectify this fact by offering a concentrated vision of advocacy that courses through every instructional decision we make in our classrooms.

To start, let us recognize that the history of advocacy in the teaching profession is as timeless as the profession itself. Advocacy is fundamentally tied to the purpose of education. The process of changing and shifting the ideas of individuals and societies is the very process of learning. Advocating is the task of entering into dialogue with an individual or group and working toward common understanding of new perspectives and beliefs. It is a process that is never neutral and that requires leaning toward and advocating for a particular goal or outcome.

Understandably, looking at the evolution of advocacy in education is to look at the history of the profession. Within the United States, organized advocacy efforts have played a fundamental role in labor rights and unionization of teachers, even though these efforts remain under siege in today's sociopolitical context. Advocacy in education tends to cluster historically around two different areas: advocating for the teaching profession and advocating for the needs of children within today's schools. Both of these contexts are incredibly important. Battles are necessarily fought for today's beleaguered teachers and students. However, both of these frames can also stymie more innovative forms of civic ingenuity and social change that could be at the heart of a more expansive vision of advocacy. By focusing narrowly on the teaching profession, the role of advocacy shifts a civic lens to primarily focus on questions of labor. Likewise, the common framing of students as ones who must be advocated for (because they cannot advocate for themselves) connotes a false generosity of do-goodery and adult benevolence for a helpless populace. While unintended, both of these outcomes reinforce a passive civic outcome vis-à-vis advocacy. This chapter seeks to turn this frame inside out. We first embrace the traditional model of advocacy *for* a profession and students as a means of orienting this civic commitment in familiar practices before expanding beyond into more innovative territory.

Recognizing the possibilities of advocacy as a central driving force in our classrooms—to engage in this practice both *for* and *with* our students—this chapter moves toward speculative dimensions of considering the land we are advocating *upon* (see Table 7.1). Offering playful, engaging, and timely approaches to taking an advocacy stance in our classroom, we continue to follow the stories of the Council of Youth Research, the Black Cloud Game, and the MS 50 debate team.

Table 7.1 Interrogating and Innovating with Advocacy

ADVOCACY LENS	WHAT TO INTERROGATE	TOOLS TO INNOVATE
Advocacy For	1. How are we supporting and addressing the learning and civic needs of the students in our classrooms? 2. How do we frame the kinds of change needed for others to act alongside us?	Framing and Core Ideas Feedback Systems

ADVOCACY LENS	WHAT TO INTERROGATE	TOOLS TO INNOVATE
Advocacy With	1. How can we center the voices and ideas of the youth we work alongside? 2. What tools can we use to examine and collect data in our efforts for civic advocacy?	Social Science Research Suite of Resources
Advocacy Upon	1. What are the more-than-human kin that inhabit the spaces we are working upon and how might we advocate alongside them? 2. What are our emotional responses to the civic inequities our (broadly interpreted) communities experiences?	Acknowledging Land Affective Check-Ins

The Importance of Civic Advocacy: Classroom and Community Contexts

Advocacy feels intuitive, and it should. We do not seek to overly complicate your understanding of what it means to be an advocate for something. As a basic definition, we understand advocating as working in support of a given outcome or change. Things do get complicated when people choose to distance themselves from the impacts of a cause. As our vision of civic imagination in this book attests to, we are writing to help guide advocacy that helps progress freedom and joy for yourself and for a collective community.

There are layers to where and how you might engage in the practice of advocating. In *Everyday Advocacy: Teachers Who Change the Literacy Narrative* (2020), English education leader Cathy Fleischer and coauthor Antero worked together to describe a kind of advocacy knowledge that we think all teachers should seek to develop in their professional practice. This work was intentionally focused on supporting the English language arts needs of students and we focused on a "little a" form of advocacy that embraced "strategies for finding their voice, taking a stand, and changing the narrative surrounding teaching, particularly around teaching literacy" (p. 6).

Echoing a central premise from *Everyday Advocacy,* teachers are positioned as natural advocates—it is at the heart of what we do. Working on behalf of the instructional goals in a classroom or a teaching profession that is often given short shrift in media and policy discussions, teachers are drivers of change through our advocacy titles. That being said, this work is often seen as outside of our in-class responsibilities. Advocacy is wonderful, the argument goes, but is something that shouldn't interfere with the standards-aligned instructional goals in a classroom. We reject this notion.

If the primary goal of classrooms is to prepare young people for meaningful civic participation outside of schools, every classroom must function as a space that can support advocacy *for* and *with* the ingenuity of young people. We are advocating for classroom advocacy.

Throughout this chapter, we want you to consider several different dimensions of advocacy. Who is advocating (e.g., who is the advocate)? What is the topic or issue being advocated for (e.g., what is the change that is being sought)? And why is this topic of immediate importance for the advocate (e.g., what is the stance of a given individual or group)? Taken together, these questions help us interrogate why advocacy is often situated as a superficial Band-Aid in some contexts today and helps us expand who is brought to the table when we are seeking change. To put it more directly, when we think critically about what we might be trying to shift within our daily practices, we might better identify and network with allies across the educational spectrum. This vision helps connect advocacy as a culminating focus of the civic lessons described throughout the prior chapters of this book.

Three Words Much Alike in Dignity

There are three interlocking words we must parse in this chapter. First, there is a verb and there is a noun and they share the same spelling:

advocate. The difference between being an advocate and advocat*ing* for someone or something is an important distinction. The action is one that can be fleeting and temporary. While you may not be forever linked as an advocate for something, the noun implies a stronger sense of permanence. Taken together, these words imply the stance of *advocacy*—supporting and working toward a particular cause. Advocacy, too, is a noun. It is one that is imbued with a state of action.

We want to distinguish these three words because the nuance is important: depending on which word is used, they speak to temporality and sustained forms of engaging around a cause and they imply how closely interwoven one's identity might be tied up in a given issue. You might sign a petition to support a local municipal measure, demonstrating that you advocate for a given change. However, that may not be an issue you are deeply connected to in longer term perspectives.

While this chapter focuses on advocacy as a stance, we want to recognize that students and teachers are approaching topics in our classrooms from a wide variety of perspectives and levels of engagement. Your form of advocacy may depend on your investment in a topic, your comfort with the ways you might be able to demonstrate your agency, and the ways you believe you can advocate safely and effectively. Advocacy is contextual.

With few exceptions, engaging in advocacy is an active process. You do something in order to advocate, be an advocate, and demonstrate a kind of advocacy. This is an important point to build upon in your classroom and one that invites critique around the kinds of activities that are otherwise centered in classrooms today. Many of our normative schooling experiences are framed around taking, interpreting, and following the rules and expectations of others in ways that stifle rather than encourage active advocacy. As we discussed in this book's introduction, civic lessons and the knowledge of federal and state-based governance help inform young people about how to adhere to a given system and how to participate in ways that are deemed safe to the ongoing preservation of the state. That is, civic imagination is staunched in schools because, taken too far, it might put stress on the levers of the democratic machine. In contrast, advocacy places action, imagination, and collaboration at the center of what someone does.

Advocacy doesn't happen to you; you don't sit around waiting to passively advocate. In this sense, it can look a lot like the kind of active learning we seek to make occur in classrooms today.

Advocacy For

When coauthor Antero and Cathy Fleischer described the kinds of classroom practices that advocate for English Language Arts (ELA) and literacy supports, we wrote about them as "little a" advocacy. This was intended to differentiate the ideas in *Everyday Advocacy* (2020) from the larger forms of organizing that the word advocacy can often convey.

But make no mistake: "little a" advocacy can lead to big changes. *Everyday Advocacy* is a testament to the results of teacher-led advocacy efforts in classrooms and for classrooms. It speaks to decades of work that Cathy has led in supporting the writing and literacy needs of legions of students and teachers across the classroom. Engaging in advocacy *for* "little a" aspects of our classrooms has positively shaped the landscape of learning and equity.

Although the rest of this chapter focuses on models of advocacy that draw in students and their families as coconspirators, we start here with the kinds of advocacy that might feel familiar and more comfortable for many readers. Speaking up for a group of students is part of what educators are guided and expected to do. Differentiated instruction, for example, is rooted in the idea that we identify and work on behalf of the varied needs of learners in our classrooms. While we are going to center the actions of teachers in this part of the chapter, we can think of no better illustration of this work in practice than young people—the Council of Youth Research—advocating for other young people.

Extending their intellectual homage to scholar Antonio Gramsci (as described in Chapter 5), the Locke High School members of the Council of Youth Research continued to explore the connections between their research and a long lineage of critical pedagogy elders. In conversation on Facebook with his teacher, one of the students, Joe, posted an explanation about the role he believed Gramsci's ideas played in his life. He reflected on a challenging moment in his school experience and how Gramsci helped illuminate ways for teachers and students to challenge the inequities faced in urban schooling settings:

Mr. Tan first asks: Can you explain a little more clearly (1) how she was being hegemonic ("how do u think gramsci wud break it down"), and (2) "how are u being counter-hegemonic??"

Joe explains: In my everyday life I feel Gramsci follows me to class. While in English I just happened to notice that the teacher was being hegemonic by telling us students that since she was the teacher, she was right. Me being the counter-hegemonic person I am, I told her that I felt she was being hegemonic and that's when she cut me off. The reason I feel this way is because if too many students were to be informed, there would be an uprising and she would lose power and in the long run lose control of the class.

Joe offers an example of a teacher at his school he believes continues to reinforce the status quo by not allowing students to voice their opinion about how the class operates. Seeing his critique of the teacher as counter-hegemonic, Joe goes on to make the point that he feels that the teacher does not believe students have something important to offer. Both Mr. Tan and Joe shift out of standard English to vernacular in order to communicate as equals, framing their topic to better communicate with one another and the other students reading these exchanges.

While not intended as a form of public advocacy, we lift this exchange from the pages of Facebook in order to illuminate Mr. Tan's approach to dialogue with his students. We also see the ways that the Council frames critical arguments as pathways for advocacy—that the very tools of action and theory are placed as interpretive lenses for understanding injustices and eventually moving to action.

Getting Started: Framing and Core Ideas.   Advocating *for*—as an approach— requires identifying and honing a proper grasp of the problem or topic being addressed.

While we're emphasizing this as advocacy for students, you do not need to toil alone in these endeavors. In fact, you cannot. Change requires the action of others around you. For example, individuals who might order the equipment you need or waive an assessment that unfairly stalls student engagement might be some of the primary targets for your advocacy efforts. You may choose to advocate for more student-choice free-reading practices in your school as opposed to assessment-driven approaches. In taking up this topic, you might draw on the powerful reading scholarship and testimony that is abundant in the field (e.g., Krashen, 2004; Miller, 2009). You are advocating *for* the needs of your students but your actions might target and be framed around administrators, parents, your department chair, or other individuals. Knowing what you are advocating for and who needs to hear your calls to action is an important and necessary step. This is such a fundamental aspect of advocacy across all of the approaches in this chapter that we offer a very deliberate task. On a sticky note (or a small piece of paper if you are as loquacious as we tend to be), list the issue you are advocating for, the ideal outcome you are working toward, and the single most important individual or group that would be most helpful in supporting your work. Here's an example:

- **Issue:** Allow students to have more ownership over their free-reading choices
- **Outcome:** Reduce the role of reading-assessment software and diagnostics in school policies
- **Target:** Assistant principal over instruction and department chair

It may be that the target you are working toward is miscalibrated. We have both had moments in our teaching careers when we went to administrators seeking to right some slight to students—a school-based policy—only to find out that the implementation came from above.

As you find out who you need to work with and who you need to compel to change, you will find yourself shifting your approach, your strategies, and your communication styles naturally. This is the kind of innate practice that we often frame linguistically as "code switching" from one register to another. Our work with the Council of Youth Research, for instance, emphasized how students will present the same data differently to their peers than they would to teachers, community members, and state officials. These are necessary accommodations, and we note this here to make clear that you have strategic choices to make in how you speak to administrators or to other teachers and we are constantly reframing and repositioning our identities as we discover whom we must advocate to and for what ends.

Throughout this discovery process, you are constantly in a state of presenting and describing what you are hoping to change. This might be a hallway conversation with another teacher and it might be a detailed PowerPoint to the district superintendent. In every context, you will need to think about the narrative you are sharing. How are you framing this story for others? This is the key tool you possess as someone who is motivated to improve the lives of young people through your civic advocacy.

As Cathy Fleisher and coauthor Antero explore in *Everyday Advocacy,* the powerful guidance of civil rights organizer Marshall Ganz (2011) is a useful resource here. Describing the general tools to utilize in literacy-based advocacy efforts, they list three core ideas to guide these actions. We briefly review all three (starting with the work of Ganz):

1. *Stories must be central.* Building from Ganz, framing our advocacy efforts around stories of a singular "self," of a collective "us," and of the current "now," Ganz emphasizes that articulating a meaningful story connected empathetically to the lived conditions of a recipient remains paramount to transformation in classrooms and schools. We acknowledge this important consideration of framing, recognizing that storytelling is a fundamental commitment we are asking of you as readers in Chapter 4.
2. *Framing an issue is crucial.* Once you can communicate the story of your issue, framing (or reframing) an issue helps locate actionable steps and desired outcomes. Rather than simply stating a well-trodden "problem" that might reinforce deficit perspectives of youth and their communities, reframing an issue allows individuals to reconsider and push against the hegemonic grain that chafes and inhibits. For example, rather than work to fight against the deep chasm of an achievement gap that cleaves students based on assessment data, you might consider reframing an argument around

what Ladson-Billings (2006) refers to as educational debt that have shaped classroom conditions across generations.

3. *Learn from grassroots models of change.* We are not doing this work from a blank slate. The great thing about being a classroom advocate in the 21st century is that there are literally centuries of powerful examples of advocacy to study and learn from. While this does not mean you have to aspire to large-scale change found in history books, it does mean considering the rhetorical, structural, and resourceful approaches to advocacy seen in the past. Likewise, long-term change takes a long time. You may spend years battling your school's approach to assessments. However, gaining an ally in this quest or finding powerful counter-data to support your claims is a huge short-term win. We encourage you to celebrate the small victories you make in the seemingly unending quest for justice in our classrooms.

These three core ideas are not definitive for all advocacy efforts. However, as a means of guiding preliminary attempts at supporting the needs in your classroom, they are a useful starting place. We expand on more inclusive forms of advocacy in the rest of this chapter. However, before fully turning toward the bringing in other perspectives, let us sit with one more familiar tool you might already rely upon in your teaching practice.

Taking It to the Next Level: Feedback Systems. How often do you solicit feedback from your students? Regardless of your answer, we think we could all probably benefit from developing even more opportunities for students to offer feedback on our teaching—both anonymous and identifiable.

As much as we appreciate the culminating course evaluations that we might conduct at the end of a semester or school year, they are often too little or too late. A major problem with course evaluations is that they typically benefit a future group. They may help you as a teacher improve your practice in the long term, but this gain is at the expense of students who did not benefit from giving you the feedback. What's more, the needs and contexts of this set of students will not necessarily hold true for your future classes. The feedback here likely will help you in the future, but this is not always the case.

Given these tensions, let's recognize what we know about the field of assessment. While end-of-unit and end-of-year summative assessments might play important roles in the current contexts of high-stakes accountability and schooling, these are not necessarily the best tools for assessing and supporting student learning. For that we need a healthy dose of formative assessments sprinkled throughout the year. The National Council of Teachers of English (NCTE) has released a powerful position statement (2013) that speaks to the importance of formative assessment to guide in-the-moment teaching and to better understand individual students' needs.

So, if we know that formative assessments allow educators to adapt and adjust to the unique needs of their students, we must also recognize that class evaluations are a kind of assessment: They reflect how a class and its individual community members are engaging with knowledge, with each other, and with the various demands of schooling. As we've explored before (e.g., Garcia & Morrell, 2022), soliciting student feedback continuously—through daily exit tickets, monthly focus groups, and the aforementioned culminating evaluations—provides you a clear insight of how the most important participants in this schooling system are responding to and engaging with your instructional decisions. However, aside from guiding you towards improvement in your practice, these mechanisms of feedback are a window into understanding where your practice, school structures, or societal issues are impeding student access to equitable learning. We want to reframe feedback as a mechanism for advocacy.

Getting useful critique can feel uncomfortable sometimes. In designing a quick form of feedback at any timescale, we encourage you to design this work around three different kinds of questions:

- What are students doing in your classroom?
- What are you as the teacher doing?
- What is the school doing?

This set of questions will allow you to see where you can improve and how you might shape your work as an advocate.

Throughout this exploration of advocating *for*, we want to be clear: we are not encouraging you to become an advocate in some misguided attempt to get your students to like you. However, when your principles within the classroom extend to your principles in how you advocate for your classroom, oftentimes these commitments will work hand in hand to build the community you are striving to create. This kind of civic synergy will spill over into the next dimension of advocacy in this chapter: advocating *with*.

Advocacy With

Throughout this book, we've focused on forms of mutuality that bind our humanity as teachers with that of our students, our community, and our shared world. Implicit in many of these practices is the use of evidence in working for the needs of a collective good. For example, when we advocate *for* our students' needs, we often bring to bear data that are familiar to the constituencies with which we are communicating. This might mean invoking assessments, flawed as they might be, to advocate for a broader range of reading materials in a classroom, demographic information to challenge perceptions of an achievement gap, or socio-economic information to broaden the material products and services available to students and families. These are all data that may be flawed and we'll still do with them what we can to work toward equitable outcomes. Conversely, while this might be a useful approach for speaking on behalf of the needs of a given community, advocating *with* should fundamentally alter our relationship to data and how we gather it.

Just as the students of the Council of Youth Research advocated *for* their own needs in the earlier part of this chapter, students can do pretty remarkable things when supported with the tools of educational research. The argumentative stances that students made were, importantly, bolstered by hefty amounts of data they scrutinized, questioned, and explicated for specific outcomes. Tellingly, most of this was data that students collected themselves. This is the primary tool to consider in this advocacy stance: the suite of mixed-methods research tools that youth can utilize.

Getting Started: Social Science Research Suite of Resources. The available tools to researchers writ large are innumerable, constantly expanding, and—often—in deep need of refinement. For example, the data generated by testing corporations for college admissions or advanced placement are tied to historical inequities and measure an individual's ability to perform on a given test rather than their knowledge or proficiency in a given topic (Au, 2009). So, while we think it is important to work with recognizable and accessible research tools (e.g., surveys, interviews, participant observation) we offer caution not to get caught up in a frenzy for data that are not immediately useful or that are extracted in ways that might lead to possible harm. Listing a few tools you might work with alongside youth of all ages and content areas, we describe below some approaches you might use.

Table 7.2 Research Methods

RESEARCH METHOD	OVERVIEW	GUIDANCE
Survey	An approach to gathering specific information from an identified group of people through predefined questions. Surveys can have fixed choices, open responses, or a mixture of both. Particularly working in educational settings, surveys can be utilized powerfully with young people to generate a large number of responses.	• What kinds of broad, demographic information might you solicit? • Are there key questions you are seeking to answer that would be better informed by *more* voices (breadth over depth)?
Interviews	Typically one-on-one conversations, interviews can create opportunities for more in-depth discussion and nuance around a given topic. For both focus groups and interviews, a set of predetermined questions—a protocol—can help ensure that a conversation stays focused on the topic at hand.	• How will you ensure that your interview participants are comfortable in this setting? • What are the kinds of questions that you will ask that get the most insight through personal recollection, opinion, and discussion (depth over breadth)?

Focus Groups	Though similar in structure and format to interviews, focus groups are ideal for creating more comfort for participants who might be clustered by affinity (e.g., students of the same grade, parents, local community activists). A focus group allows participants to build off of one another, react to other responses, and elicit insights that might not have occurred in traditional one-on-one interviews.	• How will you cluster participants for your focus group? What will you do to make sure they are comfortable discussing the topics at hand? • How will you work to draw out the voices of all of your participants in a focus group? • What is the ideal size and time length for the topic at hand?
Participant Observation	A key component of traditional ethnographic research, participant observation seeks to place research both *inside* the perspective of a given setting while also providing analytic tools for viewing this space from an *outside* stance. The seemingly contradictory nature of this approach is implied in the method's name, requiring researchers to both *participate* and to reflexively *observe*. Fieldnotes—written records of the period of observation—are the key data collected through participant observation.	• What are the ways you will *participate* within the setting you are observing? • How will others in this environment—students, employees, caregivers—react to or adjust their behavior because of your presence? • How often will you need to participate in this space to be assumed to be a regular member of this community?
Photograph/ Image/ Multimodal Analysis	The various ephemera of a school setting—from a hall pass to a yearbook to graffiti—all offer important lessons related to the research you may be conducting. Documenting, defining, and analyzing this work is a necessary component of ongoing research and taking up and inventorying this work takes time and attention.	• What artifacts in school settings might be rendered invisible through power hierarchies or day-to-day use? • How might you make the familiar artifacts of schooling *unfamiliar* through your analysis?

For all of the guidance above, the underlying question is to consider what your advocacy work needs to illuminate. What can research make clear that we might not already know or get wrong? These singular research tools are by no means definitive; we use many other forms of research tools in our work and some of these we have utilized in settings with young people. Tools like autoethnography, photovoice, and experience sampling could fill entire chapters on their own. We encourage you to look at related research work as you expand your set of research tools (see Camangian, 2009; Ozer, Ritterman, & Wanis, 2010).

Taking It to the Next Level: The Why of Advocacy. Importantly, each of these tools have rich and contested traditions. The graduate students we work with are often cautioned to distinguish between explaining a method and a methodology. While your research method might rely on a survey instrument, the theoretical considerations that shape it come from different systems of belief, conceptions of knowledge, and understanding of how that knowledge is carried and disseminated. These are often concepts framed around epistemology and ontology. This is heady stuff, but the nuance here is important: you and your students should be able to articulate why you are not only choosing to conduct interviews as a means of advocacy but why you are choosing to approach your interview and the questions you ask in a particular way. Similarly, we want you to consider the level of complexity necessary in your research design. It takes a young person's natural expertise about their lived conditions in public schooling to be able to interpret many of the questions they might ask in a survey interview. Needing to build from a validated survey instrument or calibrate their responses across a Likert scale may not be worth the time it takes to learn to meaningfully use this or other tools for any given project.

We want to emphasize that we are not saying teachers should water down the tools of research for their students. Certainly you will need to scaffold some tools and their uses for your students to wield proficiently for any given purpose. However, a fundamental premise of this approach is the recognition that youth-collected knowledge is valid and necessary for us to understand the social phenomena around us.

For the first three weeks of the Black Cloud game, students received cryptic clues—riddles, images, GPS coordinates—through hidden Pufftron sensors. These custom-made boxes measured air quality in the rooms they were placed in, uploading data to a class-specific website. As the data amassed daily, students began to see the patterns of pollution that emerge in hyperlocal settings.

As one student, Ruben, recalled, it is one thing to consider the air quality in a neighborhood "bad" and it is quite another to see that in the singular room you are sitting in, the level of carbon dioxide rises and falls based on moment-to-moment activity.

Examining the quantitative data (the level of carbon dioxide, volatile organic compounds, light, sound, and temperature), it became clear that patterns helped illuminate the behavior of air quality. Looking at the data for their own classroom, the students saw that the room got louder and quieter, darker and lighter based on the time of day. Of course, an empty classroom at night was darker and quieter than one with 40 energetic bodies crowded into it. What was also clear from the data is how 40 bodies in a room produce more heat and more carbon dioxide. Even in comparison to the local dry-cleaner and gas station, the air quality in coauthor Antero's classroom was the worst measured throughout the activity and was the worst specifically when the classroom was full of students. We were the creators of this pollution.

Students investigated and found that at the level of carbon dioxide measured, a majority of people feel drowsy or nauseated. Overcrowded classrooms create conditions for poor learning. Though students were not able to drastically change the size of classes held at their school (a fight ongoing for generations), they did get the school to provide plants and fans and encourage others to keep doors and windows open when local air conditions allowed it. This was data-driven advocacy collected through play and inquiry.

Once students have helped collect and analyze data that are meaningful for them and the civic issues driving their collective inquiries, the core principles of advocacy are, again, worth revisiting. How to frame these data for extant audiences and how to identify measurable changes to work toward and celebrate are key parts of these next steps. They require negotiating the authentic connections between youth ingenuity and the theories of change you are leveraging.

Ongoing research on project-based learning in ELA classrooms (e.g., Boardman et al., 2021; Polman, 2012) describes how contexts of instruction must align to different kinds of authenticity. Extending from the same sociocultural foundations that guide our understanding of an expansive and speculative approach to civic learning, Polman suggests that a project might consider the need for:

- *Authentic cultural tools.* Tools relied upon within an existing community. For students, we think this might be the social media networks that they naturally socialize upon or the mobile devices and apps they utilize for creative expression and personal communication.
- *Authentic community.* Students do not need to turn in homework to just an individual teacher. Rather, writing, research, and presentations might speak to people who are a part of a defined community for students (geographically, virtually, or in some other hybrid configuration).
- *Authentic personal agency.* Do students' choices and decisions in a curriculum matter? How do they know?

Ultimately, considering what feels authentic with your students—for young people and for teachers alike--requires transparency, vulnerability, and trust. Unpacking these authentic approaches to advocacy will allow students to lead as advocates with you and with each other.

Advocacy Upon

What does winning a debate round really mean? On an abstract level, a win represents a triumph of argumentation—the act of prevailing in a battle of ideas. On a practical level, it allows students to advance through a tournament and garner awards for their speaking skills and teamwork. Wins obviously validate the hours and hours of hard work that debaters put in to developing

and practicing their cases. But at the end of the day or the weekend when the tournament ends, the federal government does not
actually take up any of the policy proposals under discussion. The
academic exercise ends. Next year will bring a new topic.

The MS 50 debate team unquestionably wanted to win. Each
victory demonstrated that this traditional activity could expand
to hold multiple perspectives and alternative approaches. The
team did win many rounds, but at some point in each tournament
they would lose. Sometimes judges decided that the opposing
team made a stronger case. Sometimes judges rejected the
fundamental premises of MS 50's case. While these moments
were frustrating for the students and coaches, Principal Honoroff
continued to remind the students that they were accomplishing
something fundamentally more radical than what any win or loss
could measure—they were, if even just for an hour, altering how
other youth and adults thought about what debate could be and
what a world without borders could be. Someone might leave
the round having had their previously held beliefs challenged
and thinking a bit more creatively about immigration. When that
happened, debate could transcend the academic and become an
experience of dialogue that would not end but rather continue
crucial civic conversations.

As we have interrogated previous possibilities for advocacy as a stance
to support students or to work alongside the learners in your community, we want to acknowledge that this community encompasses
so much more than just you and the youth with whom you work. Of
course, this ecology of learners is central to our work as critical teachers; embracing our shared humanity in our classrooms is a lifelong
effort in and of itself. However, we want to consider that, even if we
were to cinch a magical lasso around the school we presently teach in,
all that ever has been and ever will be in this land extends far beyond
the gaze of just us and our students. From the nonhuman life with
which we share this land, to the legacies of anti-indigeneity reminding us that we usually teach on stolen land as uninvited guests, to
the ways this land will move and alter in accordance with the effects

of human-driven climate devastation, our schools inhabit robust multitudes.

The contexts we name above—and the many others that instantiate dread in young people from ongoing anti-Blackness to the threats of mass shootings to the lingering effects of the COVID-19 pandemic—require us to continually push for changes even from those who may be comfortable with this older, oppressive world we currently inhabit. And, while we are proponents of a speculative vision that moves us beyond the taken for granted, we want to make sure that readers are not conflating the imagined world we are working toward as lingering on some faraway horizon. Instead, when we speak of innovation that is overdue in the lives of our students and communities, we are speaking of the local relationships and freedoms around us.

Advocacy *upon* means taking up a consideration of the extremely local world. It means changing the scale of change from hyperconnected and global to an intentional scrutiny of the local. Of course, these two contexts—the global and the local—are bound with one another. When your phone blinks a recurring notification about a mass shooting in another part of the country, that gut punch of grief is felt in the here and now. It takes a tremendous amount of privilege, resources, and deliberation to actively turn off the extant world. This is not the kind of advocacy we are speaking toward. Instead, this focused stance of advocacy upon the land we inhabit is a reminder to attune ourselves to the conditions of the present moment. To remember a beating "why" when it comes to social change that thumps in each of our chests.

If it is not clear by now, the focus on this local advocacy means learning to be an advocate for yourself. As a reminder, your local ecosystem includes you. If you are not working toward your own health, betterment, and social and spiritual growth, you are molding in place with the environment around you.

During the first year of the pandemic, coauthor Antero cohosted weekly virtual gatherings for the National Council of Teachers of English alongside Dr. Detra Price-Dennis. These were spaces for English teachers to check in about how they were feeling and what they were doing to support themselves through a time of unprecedented turmoil and stress. We started each gathering with a set of recurring questions: Where are you? How are you? What's your balm?

Many of our professional development resources, trainings, and books assume we are these benevolent sources, unfeeling and unmoved from the sentiments and issues in our classrooms or the world. Every one of you reading this book knows this is not the case.

As Antero has explored (Garcia, 2019), rather than actually treating this healing gap between teachers' emotions and the heaviness of what we are often expected to address for our students, much of the rhetoric around teachers is focused on self-care. While we believe it is important to care for oneself and to do so as a form of advocacy, we do not think that simply targeting self-care at the individual level should lead us to ignore that the exacerbated need for relief is arising because our systems of labor are failing to offer meaningful support.

If we recognize the importance of being tuned in to our feelings of the world around us, we might better communicate our own needs and desires. We might see that the murky cloud of sadness that shadows my teaching is one that hovers over many of us. As coauthor Nicole (2018) argues, understanding your own needs means you might build toward a shared civic empathy with your colleagues.

Getting Started: Acknowledging Land. Let's return to the first question we asked teachers during those NCTE gatherings: Where are you? Coauthor Antero and Detra framed this question to be considered mentally and emotionally. This question also speaks to the physical land upon which we are resting. It has become customary in many presentations to begin with a land acknowledgement—a recognition that the land on which we speak and hold space is usually not our own. That it is stolen native land, and we act as uninvited guests. If you are curious about whose land you are presently on and would like to learn more, there are a plethora of resources available to you. At the time that we write this, https://native-land.ca/ is an easy site to quickly explore.

Of course, simply acknowledging the inequitable nature of inhabiting stolen land is not enough, and we are wary that such acknowledgments can become performative when not tied to advocacy or rematriation. We are not offering a blanket set of suggestions on how you understand whose land you inhabit or the consequences. However, we do want to offer the broad recognition of acknowledgment as an initial step toward advocacy. Your civic commitments cannot end with the head nod of seeing an injustice. We look to broaden our scope of who and what else might be sharing space with us in any given moment.

Taking It to the Next Level: Affective Check-Ins. As we work to sense and feel our way upon the land we inhabit, we can attune ourselves to the obvious fact that it is full of life that isn't human. From family pets to local wildlife—birds, raccoons, rodents—to the flora that fights to breathe alongside school asphalt, our civic commitments include much more than just human thriving.

Even naming the needs that get clouded out in our human pursuits is a start. Constructing housing for those in need often means devastating the ecologies of the nonhuman life dwelling in the ground and uprooting trees. While our progress will not always move hand in hand with the nature around us, we can begin to consider how our actions might advocate for more-than-human experience and thriving. Building from the tools described in this chapter and in other portions of this book, what are the stories that might be told by the dandelions in your schoolyard? What new insights might be solicited if interview questions were crafted from the perspective of the wildlife that subsists on the food waste at your school? How might your civic networks expand if you were to draw an asset map of the nonhuman life around you?

These are both playful provocations and actual questions we hope you and your community work toward answering. As we work toward civic innovation through our advocacy efforts, our historical relationship on land we share inequitably with others offers new opportunities for exploring, dreaming, and imagining.

Advocacy Amid Complicity

This is a scary time to be a student. At the time that we write this, the threats facing young people in this country feel heavy, insurmountable, and punishingly incomprehensible. From climate devastation that causes ongoing feelings of dread to continued inaction in this country around mass shootings, life in America is filled with reminders that the current crop of adults has done little to mitigate the threats to young people's livelihoods.

Arguably, not only have adults as a collective punted on acting toward any kind of meaningful response to the existential ongoing threats to humanity, but also adults in schools have specifically reinforced this inaction. In our own exploration of the speculative possibilities of civic action in classrooms—as noted throughout this book—we are reminded that perhaps schools are complicit in the mess we are in presently. We are not just saying we must advocate because we are complicit in the mess that young people are inheriting from us. Rather, we are advocating for and with students and upon a community that binds our lives with theirs.

In *Everyday Advocacy* (2020), Cathy and coauthor Antero describe four ways to strategize in your advocacy efforts. Teachers need to be "smart"—developing a deep knowledge about the issue and contexts you are working within. Next, teachers need to be "safe"—seeking to make changes in ways that rely on allies and work within the confines of comfort in your setting. Teachers need to be "savvy"—moving from ideas to action means learning to work within and across the rules of a system. Finally, this work must be "sustainable" (p. 40). This last word is the one we want to uplift here. It is not enough to see advocacy as a one-and-done approach. The project-based learning activity in your classroom or student-led inquiry activity? That's not gonna cut it. Instead, how do you make your commitment a part of your everyday activity? What do you do to transform your daily activities to be commensurate with your work as an advocate?

Discussion Questions

1. What are the ways you can begin advocating *for* student needs in your existing school context? What barriers have you faced in the past and who might help you?
2. As you consider the research tools at hand in your setting and your own disciplinary expertise, how can you make advocating *with* your students a fundamental part of your classroom practice?

3. How might you make the land your school setting inhabits a key consideration in your advocating work?

4. As you continue to work toward new approaches for advocating with and for students, what are the ways you might frame issues in order to build allyship and guide others to act on the needs you are illustrating?

Chapter 8

|| | | | | | | | | | | | | | | | | |

Bringing It All Together: Planning for the World to Come

We return to a common refrain in each of the previous chapters; namely, that schools are not currently designed to support the flourishing of the expansive civic commitments needed to build new worlds. We have reviewed the multiple ways that the logics of schooling socialize us educators into narrowing our vision of the possible, reducing the scope of our goals, and minimizing the potential of ourselves and our students. Realizing that we are acted upon by forces outside of our conscious control—and that those forces have influenced us to act in ways contrary to the best interests of young people and democracy—can certainly stir up feelings of discomfort. We cannot count the number of times we winced while writing this book as we reflected upon past choices we made in the classroom that contradicted our values.

We must not allow our unavoidable complicity within traditional educational structures to guilt us into inaction. When we know better, we do better. Change is not only possible; it's necessary. It is difficult, no doubt, but we can unlearn some of our socialization and embrace the humility, curiosity, and grace to act in the service of a more just and equitable world to come.

Much of this unlearning takes place through our planning practice: the painstaking and complex process through which we translate our political values and ethics into units, assignments, and daily lesson plans. Just as our teaching practice manifests influences from a range of sources—from our preparation programs to our continuing professional development to district or school mandates—so, too, does our planning. Some of us have complete free rein over our curriculum while others are constrained by scripted lessons; some of us have access to a range of resources while others are restricted to what is available in the supply closet or book room. Whatever our circumstances, we can take steps to integrate world-building commitments into planning for our disciplinary instruction. Following the model established in previous chapters, we can start with small moves and then take it to the next level when we feel ready.

This chapter synthesizes the resources offered throughout the book by offering a planning template intended to support you in translating the ideas generated from the commitments into practice in your unique context. We also share stories from some teachers you have gotten to know throughout this book. Members of the 3D Project teacher team discuss their own world-building journeys to demonstrate the different possible entry points and outlets for this work.

Planning Template

We often tell our preservice teacher candidates that unit planning is always a bit of a dance. We are strong proponents of the backward design model, in which the establishment of culminating goals guides the choice of curricular resources and the development of daily lessons; indeed, we bristle when students tell us they are designing units around discrete disciplinary concepts or texts (e.g., my fractions unit or my *To Kill a Mockingbird* unit). "Hold on!" we plead. Why is an understanding of fractions or of particular texts important for understanding and acting upon the world in which we live—and the world we hope to build? This is not a rhetorical or sarcastic question. The responses represent the building blocks of a meaningful unit plan. If we cannot think of an engaging answer to that question then we know we need to rethink our unit altogether. Understanding the big ideas we want to play with should dictate the materials and flow of lessons we develop.

Yet we cannot ignore the fact that we operate amid a variety of constraints. Perhaps we are required to teach a fractions unit due to school or district mandates. Perhaps *To Kill a Mockingbird* is the text available in the book room. This is where the pragmatic dance begins as we toggle back and forth between what we want to do, what we are required to do, and what we have the resources to do. Rather than moving in linear fashion from big ideas toward day-to-day activities, we bounce around in our planning to make what we have at our disposal work in the service of our idealistic goals. Even if we do not have the freedom to build units out of whole cloth, we can still make adjustments in order to patch together learning experiences that take disciplinary learning to that next world-building level.

While every teacher's planning process and constraints will differ slightly, we suggest that playing with the following elements in this template can jump-start your instructional imagination (see Table 8.1).

Table 8.1   Planning Template

Essential Question(s):
Civic Literacy Skill(s):
Integration of World-Building Principles: (one or more)

Formative/ Summative Assessment(s):	___ Real World Topics	___ Civic Dialogue
	___ Authentic Audience	___ Community Action

Text Set: **Fiction** (Novels, short stories, poems, drama)

Non-Fiction (Newspaper/magazine/blog articles, speeches, informational texts)

Multimedia (Film clips, online content, podcasts)

Authors (Diversity of gender, race, age, country of origin, ability status, sexual orientation)

What do students need to know and be able to do in order to successfully complete the summative assessment?
How might they need to think or act differently?

Content:	Skills:

Classroom Activities: (Begin daily lesson planning here)

Essential Questions

In Chapter 3 we introduced the idea that organizing instruction around big, thorny questions that have no easy answers imbues teaching and learning with a spirit of inquiry. The knowledge and skills in every discipline apply to real-world issues, controversies, or ethical dilemmas; drawing those out with students is not only an engaging method of instruction but also takes seriously the status of students as developing civic leaders who will need to wrestle with the implications of what is being learned. When coauthor Nicole returned to the English classroom after coordinating the Council of Youth Research, she was assigned to teach 11th-grade American Literature classes. Inspired by the principles of YPAR, she rejected a chronological tour of great books and instead organized the course thematically around a yearlong essential question: What are the possibilities and tensions we face in this American life? Each unit featured an inquiry question highlighting a different tension—majority and minority rights, freedom and security, citizenship and consumerism—that folded into community inquiry projects designed by the students. What are the juicy questions in your field that you can invite your students to explore?

Civic Literacy Skills

Another strategy offered in Chapter 3 involved a shift in how we think about standards, from indicators of narrow academic competencies to indicators of authentic actions in civic life. Every discipline has both content and skill standards: what students need to know and what they need to be able to do with that knowledge. Across the disciplines the skill standards are grounded in literacy in the form of reading; writing; listening or speaking as a historian, a mathematician, or a scientist; and so on. We remember clearly the mandates we were given by our previous administrators to ensure that every lesson was standards-based and that the daily standards (or at least their corresponding numbers) were written on the white board each day. These requirements made reviewing the standards more of a pesky chore for us than a useful grounding for our practice; the message is to just find one that fits. We reinvigorated our use of standards by reminding ourselves that they are meant to stand in for activities in which students should be able to engage outside of the classroom. Using the term "civic literacy skill" takes us out of the abstract land of standards and grounds us in what we hope students will be able to do with our lessons. For instance, let's take an example of a Common Core reading standard in our discipline of English Language Arts (ELA): "Determine a central idea of a text and analyze its development over the course of the text." Rather than simply adding to our lesson or unit plans, we analyze why this reading skill is important for students in their understanding of the world. We translate this into a civic literacy skill by considering that citizens need to understand the nature of the positions expressed through media about issues of public concern and the strategies used by media producers to justify those positions. This is a subtle shift but one that reminds us to communicate with students about why they should learn what we are teaching.

Integration of World-Building Principles

As we discussed in Chapter 1, world building is an inherently messy and aspirational project, and there is no blueprint or step-by-step guide for how to do it. Even our articulation of the five world-building civic commitments is a bit of an artificial construction because in practice the concepts are inextricably linked and impossible to tease apart. Nonetheless, we find the commitments valuable as tools to support thinking and planning. Importantly, the commitments are not cumulative; you are not doing more or better world building the more commitments you address in a unit. Instead, you may find that particular topics lend themselves to deeper exploration of one or two commitments and that a school year may give you the opportunity to cycle through many of them. You can make the choice to explicitly discuss the commitments with your students or instead to implicitly fold them into the choices you make about assessments and texts.

Formative or Summative Assessments

Some of the most powerful tools at our disposal to transform our curriculum and instruction are our assessments—what we ask our students to do to showcase their learning. If we change the way we think about assessments, we believe we can fundamentally change the tenor and purpose of our teaching. We can break down the classroom walls and dismantle the artificial boundaries between schools and communities when we ask students to demonstrate what they have learned in their disciplines through application in authentic outlets. To awkwardly remix the old adage, if students complete an assignment and only the teacher is there to hear it, does it really make a sound? Connecting our assessments to real audiences and actions prods us to make explicit linkages between our content, the world as it is, and the world as it could be. The planning template offers several potential options for developing new assessments or tweaking old ones. This list is certainly not exhaustive; again, the goal is not to check every box but rather to reflect on the messages your assignments send to students about the aims of education.

Text Sets

The curriculum inventory in Chapter 3 suggested that taking a critical eye to the resources we utilize to introduce elements of our disciplines to students can help us to identify potential biases or gaps in our instruction. The inventory can act as a powerful lever for expanding our curriculum in ways that embrace political values of justice and equity. We conceptualize text in the broadest possible sense here to represent all of the materials and resources that we bring to bear in our practice. We suggest that attending to the categories of genre, modality, and voice can serve to diversify the range of experiences that students encounter in our classes. In keeping with Chapter 4's focus on storytelling, we suggest a place for fiction across the curriculum—not only in ELA classes—as an engine for creative and imaginative takes on subject matter. Similarly, a nudge toward integration of text other than print offers not only multiple content access points for students but also a higher chance of more participatory, up-to-the-moment, and innovative takes on relevant public issues. The variety of voices brought to bear on the understanding of important issues encourages expansive forms of perspective-taking on the part of both authors and students and has the potential to add grace, nuance, and empathy to our approach to public decision making.

We know there is a difference between reading a template in the abstract and truly grasping how practicing educators put it into action within the complex contexts of their own classrooms. As a result, we invited teachers who embrace world-building civic education in their practice to share how they approach planning with the commitments of inquiry, storytelling, networking, imagination, and advocacy in mind. You know them a bit by now: They are members of the 3D Project teacher team. Christina, Peter, Janelle, and Molly engaged in dialogue and writing with us in the hopes of offering a different form of grounded guidance for engaging in this work.

Christina: Translation and Resilience

Coauthor Nicole: What processes do you engage in to translate the world-building commitments and philosophy you have for education into your everyday planning of curriculum and instruction?

Christina: When I started teaching, I went to weekly meetings of the Philadelphia Teachers' Learning Cooperative where we created together and also practiced the descriptive review process popularized by Patricia Carini (as described in Cushman, 1997). The ways of looking at student work and my own practice have become roots for strong world building, storytelling, inquiry, networking, and advocacy. The descriptive review process resists narrow and often deficit-based views of students (e.g., focusing only on reading or proficiency levels) in order to move teachers toward recognizing and incorporating student interests, passions, modes of thinking, and relationships with others into the curriculum. Because I seek to know my students in this way, world building by necessity looks different for each student. World building happens internally, with deep dives into imagination, criticality, emotions, leadership, and abiding connections. World building also happens with an outward gaze through engaging with book worlds that open up new spaces, places, and people. Because I commit to see students' work through a descriptive inquiry lens, I strive to see where the next moves might be— sometimes making worlds bigger or smaller—without pushing too hard too fast.

This inquiry stance also makes me more understanding of myself as a teacher–learner. I give myself room to take risks. I work in liminal spaces with colleagues. I show students I am learning, too. This year that has involved collaboration with students and other teachers to plan school wide wellness days where students get to imagine what they'd like to do during the day and collectively facilitate those experiences.

From my work with Teachers Learning Cooperative, I have a strong commitment to making and creating. I see my curriculum as a made thing and I see school wide events we plan together as made things—objects with our marks on them, our hands in them. I see classroom discussions as a made thing, the classroom itself becoming more and more a space made by the community. This year, during creative writing, I had a student writing Peppa Pig [cartoon character] fanfic (they were interactive slides, actually, and quite amazing). I brought in some Peppa Pig toys that I found for free on local neighborhood swap sites so students could create tableaus. Other students brought in little figurines as well and it became a common practice; the windowsill had changing tableaus with childhood toys that reflected the season (they made a winter camping scene with campfires made out of paper bags and flames and smoke and sparks made out of beads. Another student brought in these cool, mini winter-decorated toy RVs). All of this is to say that seeing the classroom as a made thing means imagination, world building, and storytelling can all converge on my windowsills. This same kind of imagination, world building, and storytelling happens when I network with colleagues and partners to create schoolwide projects. When my colleagues and I make with each other and with our students for the community, the things we make reflect our imagination in the moment and a belief in our ability to pull it off.

Peter's Story

Nicole: What keeps you going when you feel the constraints of the world as it is getting in the way of your civic dreaming with your students? What gives you the resilience to reach out to partners instead of retreating inward?

Peter: My students keep me going. I am a teacher. I love young people and feel like they need to be happy and safe and equipped (intellectually, emotionally, and mentally) for the often horrible world that they live in and awaits them outside (and unfortunately sometimes inside) our school walls. Kids and their future is why I wake up every morning and head into a very difficult teaching environment for little pay and, seemingly, less respect. All youth should have the opportunity to grow and flourish safely and successfully regardless of color or race or gender or sexuality or income level.

Fight or flight is an instinct. Many species encounter and

determine risks and make decisions based on observation about what is best for them. I do retreat inward sometimes, and I think that is okay. It is a flight, but I see it oftentimes as a chance to regroup to put up the fight. Sometimes, I just need to get myself in the right headspace. Sometimes, I need to hammer out for myself what is going on: good or bad. That way, I feel like I am a detective solving my own mysteries: arming myself with the appropriate evidence and tools to continue on.

There are times when I can figure it all out by myself, while other times, I need a lot of support. That is when I reach out. I have several families in my world that include some close colleagues in my building, teachers I know throughout my county (in particular through the Oakland Writing Project), and really strong teachers from across the country who I have met doing various initiatives or programs. I know that any and all of these people will have my back and help me problem solve anything I come across. I am a smart person, and they are even smarter, so collectively, we are brilliant. To continue the whole fight metaphor, these are my armies—big and small.

One example comes to mind from a couple of years ago. We teach an 11th-grade memoir unit in 11th grade at my school. I noticed that the mentor texts were skewed—written predominantly by white authors and women authors. This didn't sit well with me because students were not encountering a range of perspectives—particularly ones that better reflected their own identities. After having conversations with some of my colleagues in the county, someone recommended a perfect piece: "Just Walk On By—Black Men and Public Space" by Brent Staples, an African American author. It was perfect for my students, many of whom have witnessed or experienced exactly what Staples wrote about. It was relevant to them and their lives. It allowed them to see themselves reflected in the author's words. It helped them know that their story can matter as well. Sometimes colleagues can help you see small tweaks that can transform your practice.

Janelle's Story:
Pandemic as Portal to World Building

Janelle: After a full year and a half of virtual learning, my learners craved connection. At the 9th-grade level, many social learning milestones were missed due to quarantine. As the 2021–2022 school year began, it was essential for me to reorganize and rethink how the year would work with the intention of addressing students' social and emotional needs. One thing was clear for sure: no meaningful learning would take place without community-building. My students hadn't had a routine of seeing trusted adults who were not their parents, their friends, new acquaintances, or even those who challenged or questioned them. They simply were out of practice being with others. Early on, I knew world-building civic skills would be crucial in creating and sustaining a learning community.

"This year, we will get back to normal. We will not have the limits as we did during Covid. We will return to in-person instruction, extracurricular activities, and field trips."

That was the message of August 2021 as we planned for the new school year. The sentiment was clear: let's return to a school year that was as normal as possible. But here's the deal: as much as we wanted to offer young minds the rigorous, uninterrupted, face-paced, get-them-ready-for-testing curriculum of before Covid, there was no denying that Covid happened. Covid happened and is happening, and it served us all a generous slice of humble pie with a huge dollop of trauma right on top.

My call-to-action essential question for the year: How do we learn deeply and meaningfully in collaborative communities while healing from trauma?

Certainly, the pandemic turned our world upside down. Homes became workplaces. Zoom calls replaced get-togethers. Bedrooms became classrooms. Boundaries were blurred, revised, redrawn, abolished, redrawn again. This wasn't just because of Covid—there were (and are) several traumatic events that have forced us to rethink our place in society. Over and over again this past year, I was reminded of my community's most pressing need: attending to mental and social-emotional health. This need quickly unfolded into a civic call to action for me as I witnessed countless instances of stress, anxiety, and uncertainty. But, how might we get closer to a reality that promotes healing?

What might that look like? This year required imagination, flexibility, and purpose—all framed by a familial sense of closeness.

JANELLE'S STORY: INQUIRY: JUMPING RIGHT IN

We got off to a messy, slow, and difficult start. At my school, it is a tradition to begin the school year with a grade-level first-week project. This year was no different. I find it to be a good idea to begin the year with clear expectations of what project-based learning is and what a project looks like from launch to postfinal presentation reflection.

Our 9th grade first-week project has long involved freshmen working in groups to create time capsules that they will open in their senior year. Continuing traditions is vital in any organization to support bonding over shared learning, community, and culture, but it's also important to constantly update these rituals. It quickly became clear that students were at a different starting point this year. As they reflected on what type of learner they are, shared their interests, and designed their capsule together, there were inescapable notes of anxiety, awkwardness, attention-seeking, and disengagement sprinkled across every group. It wasn't about the content; it was the working with, the asking of, and the lack of trust or confidence in their teammates and in themselves.

They knew the most recent years were full of grace and perhaps inconsistent expectations due to virtual learning. They understood what they were being asked to do, but it was almost as if they had forgotten how to do school. More precisely, they had experienced a year and a half of school during which when and how they did their work didn't really matter. Much of it had to do with them needing social interaction above everything else. As the year began, my learners wondered:

- How do I do school?
- How can I balance socializing with responsibilities?
- Why is school important? What difference does it make?

And so as the year progressed, I continued to investigate alongside them:

- How can I build social skills into my curriculum?
- How does education make a difference in people's lives?
- How do I heal while helping others to do the same?

JANELLE'S STORY: NETWORKING: PLAYING TOGETHER PART 1

Just as I needed to get to know my students, they needed to get to know one another. We have this structure at our school called Flex Fridays. Teachers and learners design their own schedules for the day. It's an opportunity for students to get extra support, make up missing assignments, explore different interests, have whole-grade meetings, presentations, etc.

The intention is to have all community members design or even facilitate sessions. I simply invited learners to write sessions they wanted on the board so I could share these ideas with my colleagues. Their suggestions included: knitting, soccer, games, plants, food, and creative writing.

I have always hosted yin yoga sessions to help with the overall well-being of my students and foodie flex to provide some practical life skills. This year, I added the Ted Lasso Club (inspired by the television show) for 5 on 5 soccer and GROW club.

I had planned to only offer the soccer flex session occasionally because, quite honestly, I had no expertise in the sport other than watching the fantastic show! New teams were formed. Learners across grade levels worked together, competed, found new friends, or reconnected with old ones. If not for this flex session, they would either have to hope to earn a spot on one of the school or community teams or just wait until they had time, place, and no other obligations.

With a nudge from learners, this need to play was fulfilled during school hours. The response was overwhelming. I had forgotten it may have been two years since the last time they met in a park for a pick-up game. I had overlooked the idea that when I started sponsoring this flex, learners would sign up to make up for all the missed games due to quarantine. Week after week, 30–45 participants were waiting to play, waiting to compete with their team (old or new), waiting to cheer one another on. It is now a steady, expected, well-attended session.

JANELLE'S STORY: IMAGINATION: PLAYING TOGETHER PART 2

Students weren't the only ones who missed camaraderie and play. Educators missed being able to plan and facilitate meaningful community projects. In some ways, being socially distanced resulted in newfound energy and creativity. Projects that spanned multiple grade levels were always something that many of us on my campus aspired to, but the logistics alone made bringing these projects to fruition seem like a pipe dream. This year, however, was different. The English department capitalized on the multiple readings of Shakespeare that students traditionally engaged in as they progressed through high school as a moment to collaborate and create something relevant and student-centered. We all took a planning day together to brainstorm, create fliers, and set expectations for the event. We wanted every learner to develop their particular grade's part of what we called Shakespeare in the Perk (mmm, coffee!).

So what does Shakespeare look like across grade levels? For freshmen, it was a Love and Hate Exhibit in which groups designed their own interactive response to Romeo and Juliet. They created an escape room, a Bachelorette-style show, gardens with plants representing characters and conflicts, a rap battle, an art exhibit, dresses designed to symbolize love and hate, and many more—all presented for evaluation by members of the community. For the sophomores, it was rewriting and performing a variety of plays in various genres or contexts. The 10th-graders

also hosted the coffee house portion of the event. Juniors analyzed the Seven Deadly Sins through Shakespeare texts. Seniors
explored anything but Shakespeare as they read chosen Hogarth
adaptations and created short films based on the texts.

All of the learner-designed products were presented at an
evening event. Hundreds of people attended. It was a wonderful time for the campus to interact with the community and the
students thrived on sharing their work and ideas with a wider
audience. Our department made our cross–grade level project dream come true. We understood our own need to design
something new, offer creative yet rigorous opportunities to our
learners, and celebrate their work with our community.

JANELLE'S STORY: ADVOCACY: SLAMMING FOR A CAUSE

Years ago during a speech to members of my school network,
physician Abdul El-Sayed shared his story of learning while healing from trauma. Part of his analysis was that in order to heal, you
need to find purpose in what you're doing, know your own story
is important, and work with others toward a common goal. This
year, a poetry slam that we've done for years took on new meaning as an opportunity for healing and civic engagement.

I was so very sad that COVID-19 interrupted our school's project, Slamming for a Cause, in 2021. This project has long been a
turning point for many of our freshmen. There's something about
researching global human rights violations, crafting a slam poem
as a call to action, workshopping with Dallas Poet Laureate, Joa-
quin Zihuatanejo, designing marketing materials, hosting the
event, bake sale, and silent auction—all while advocating for their
chosen local nonprofit, Dallas Children's Advocacy Center (a local
organization providing legal support, safe places, and mental
healthcare to children who are victims or witnesses of abuse)—
that joyfully challenges and unites a group. Admittedly, this is
traditionally a successful and rewarding project. The previous
class in 2020 raised over $11,000 for their chosen nonprofit and
had so many attendees that we needed to move to a larger space.

This year, we needed to set goals but be mindful of the current climate. We considered new challenges: people still reluctant to attend in-person events, possible scrutiny due to sensitive topics, lack of support from businesses and bidders due to economic impact from the pandemic, learners and staff still reeling from returning to school. These real-world tensions needed careful planning and creativity, but we could not let these fears stop us.

Instead, we listened to our learners' ideas: We could live stream the event for people who are not local or don't feel comfortable coming; we could contact the most expensive hotel in town and see if they can help; we could invite our middle school teachers; we could have a booth at our local farmers' market; we could sell savory food and not just sweets; we could have flex sessions to help us plan and make items to sell; we could have social media people in charge of sharing where we are in relation to our goal. We took up every single one of these suggestions. I don't know if it was these suggestions or their excitement at us taking their suggestions seriously, or a combination, but the event shattered all expectations.

Learners set a fund-raising goal of $12,000. They reached that goal days before the event. They set a new goal of $15,000. They beat that goal before the event as well. They set a final goal of $18,000. With bake sale, ticket, T-shirt, and auction sales, the class of 2025 raised over $24,000 for the Dallas Children's Advocacy Center. The new location—the gym—was standing room only. Poets had discovered their voices. Learners understood how every tweet, every email, every call, every conversation championed their cause. Most of all, freshmen understood the work they did in school made a huge impact on others inside and outside of school.

JANELLE'S STORY: STORYTELLING: MY STORY IS WORTH SHARING

While understanding how to share stories to garner support for those that need it is important, there was another important step. Learners needed to understand they, too, had stories that should be told. Their interests mattered. Their stressors mattered. The lessons they learned mattered.

As their culminating project, freshmen were invited to write, present, and film TED-Ed Talks. I asked them to discuss what sparked excitement in their lives. Many weren't comfortable doing this either because they didn't think their interests were important or because they weren't accustomed to being asked this at school. I further urged them to express why they thought this played such an important role. Topics explored included: what makes someone intelligent, the healing power of art, how knitting helped me socially, the history of utensils, the importance of not watering a dead tree, caring for my grandmother who has dementia, and how I want to reinvent myself. Some very interesting topics, right?

When they went further to discuss what they gained from the process or how it shaped their lives, that's when the good stuff really happened. Their reflections indicated a common thread of tending to a positive sense of self. Conclusions like, "I am more than my grades," "People think I'm a bad person, but I want to help others," "I can no longer be there for someone who will not do the same for me," "Whenever you talk to someone, just know they, too, have a story," "It is important for me to take time to do the things I enjoy" shook me to my core. I wasn't expecting them to be so self-aware, but they were. I wasn't expecting them to make such profound connections, but they did. I wasn't expecting them to share such vulnerable stories, but they did so proudly. I wasn't expecting any of this, but I dreamed of it. I hoped for it. I imagined it could happen. And it did.

Lessons learned:

- We can do hard things.
- It is easier to imagine a different world when there are parameters set in this world.
- Playing together isn't just for the learners.

Molly's Story: Adventurous Civility

My reflections on today's civic landscape—the polarization of politics, the vitriol of social media, the digging in of heels, the certainty of being right—inspired me to find a way to teach my students how to talk across differences.

I had taught *The Autobiography of Malcolm X* for many years and knew that it held the capacity to challenge some of my white students' beliefs about living in a racialized world. This book always challenges them to see their experiences through different eyes. For some, this shift becomes too much to handle, leading to the danger of disengagement; for others, it instills curiosity and commitment to see the world from alternative perspectives. My students from racially minoritized communities would often express a sense of validation as they read. Much of their writing and reflection about the book revolved around a sense of viscerally understanding his experiences with racism and resulting distrust of white people.

I felt that I could do a better job of not only supporting my white students to explore perspectives different from their own, but also validating and expanding the experiences of my students of color.

Then I happened upon journalist Krista Tippett's *On Being* podcast; specifically, an episode in which two people who held polar opposite views were invited to engage in a vulnerable conversation about a contentious civic issue—in this particular case, on the topic of abortion. I became intrigued and felt that this tapped into the fundamental role of education: to help students to hold a connection with a person who feels deeply different than themselves about a subject and to manage that paradox carefully.

The magic of Tippett's moderation of the conversation is the way she allows each party to share their worldview; specifically, how their experiences with the world developed their beliefs. I came to understand that when we offer this sharing, what becomes centered is not the issue itself but the way the person has come to the belief. This is what allows the conversation to blossom—the knowledge that the goal is not necessarily to change anyone's mind, but rather, to understand the person's worldview and how their belief came to be.

Why is this important? Because I believe that in our day-to-day lives we will change no one's minds if we are polarized and disconnected. Once we can hold conversation and feel a connection, we become liberated from the belief and into relationship.

So I researched the Grounding Virtues of Tippett's On Being Project (Tippett, 2022) and taught them to my students. These virtues became our classroom agreements and I used them as a foundation to build thinking and community trust:

- Words that Matter
- Hospitality
- Humility
- Patience
- Generous Listening
- Adventurous Civility

The focus for the Malcolm X unit became Adventurous Civility—the ability to hold a conversation with a person with whom we disagree about a public issue. We examined *The Autobiography of Malcolm X* through the lens of his shifts of worldview throughout the book. Students picked a worldview that they felt shifted in each section of the book and then found evidence to support their thinking.

Midway through the book, as students gained comfort with the concept of worldview, they began to explore their own worldviews concerning different issues to begin to understand how they had formed their opinions through the influence of their upbringing and the society in which they live.

Once they landed on an issue and explored where their own opinion came from, they began to plan for their own Civil Conversation—a conversation with someone who held a different opinion on that issue. The goal was to understand how that person's worldview had shaped their opinion rather than "winning" the discussion. Oh . . . and . . . students filmed these discussions so they could later analyze the conversation moves they made to allow their partner to open up.

Over the last three years of completing this assignment, I have had students discuss their belief (or lack of belief) in God with a parent who deeply believes, abortion issues with girl-friend/boyfriend, dating concerns with a father, curfew issues with parents, and even more mundane issues such as comparing Chipotle to Qdoba. The point is that students find their own entry points where they take a risk but choose a topic they feel confident to discuss with another person.

I have students write to me often telling me that this unit is the one they draw upon the most in their day-to-day lives because they often come into contact with people they disagree with. In our landscape of polarization, it seems to me that having a conversation is way better than what most adults are modeling right now: simply shutting down.

Your Turn: Questions to Jumpstart Your Planning

1. Reflect upon the five world-building civic commitments and let your mind wander a bit. How do each of them resonate with you and where could you see openings to integrate them into your practice?
2. Describe a unit, assignment, or project (e.g., one that you are required to teach or one that you developed yourself) you could revise or change to bring it more in line with your commitments and with your students' needs.
3. What scaffolds do you need to translate the world-building commitments and philosophy you have for education into your everyday planning of curriculum and instruction?
4. What supports can you turn to (or create) when you feel the constraints of the world as it is getting in the way of civic dreaming with your students? What can give you the resilience to reach out to partners instead of retreating inward?

Chapter 9
||||||||||||||||

Conclusion: I Hesitate,
But I Do Have Hope

I hate to speak up. I get really nervous when I have to talk. And every time I speak, I try to find some motivation. And normally, for me, the best motivation is from anger.

All weekend, my whole motivation's been coming from the conversation we had last night, where we talked about Roosevelt [High School]. As wealthy as this country is, we have a 14 trillion dollar gross domestic product. In every city that I go to, schools that serve the poor, poor schools are shitty, not because we are a poor nation, but because we treat them that way. And the motivation is not to yell at somebody else to do something about it. The motivation is "What do I do?" When you look in the mirror now, "What do I do?"

The one piece of advice is to be strong. If you are strong and you are righteous, you cannot be defeated. Frederick Douglass said that "You can take away my liberty, but you can't take away my freedom because I own that." And it's the same way with your power. People may take it away physically, they may take it away materially, but existentially, they can't touch you. Be strong. Be strong when you speak, be strong when you respond to questions, but just be strong because people are counting on us. There's so much to do. There are Roosevelts all over the country.

Now, you have something that you have to offer and that's your intellect. You see, the most potent weapon in the hand of the oppressor is the mind of the oppressed. But the mind of a revolutionary is a more potent weapon than that.

It's your intellect.

We fight with words, because words become action. And that's how you do it. This is just one step amongst many steps.

It's sad because it's the last time we're going to be together as this group. But this group is destined to do great things, if you stay strong and if you stay righteous, because right is on your side.

It's about communicating to people.

I want people to feel outraged. We've done all that, "Oh, you guys are beautiful and you're smart and what not." Outrage. But empowerment. Outrage and empowerment leads to hope.

I'm angry. But you've given me something to do with that. We see what happens in our communities because people are angry. But no one has given them something to do. Another Che quote: "The difference between a gang and an army is vision." Take that outrage and turn it into something. This is what you can do. If you're feeling bad, as you're sitting in this comfortable seat, in this nice bougie convention center in the middle of Denver, then this is what you do.

This is what you do. Take it to them.

Let's go.

—Ernest Morrell (personal communication, 2011)

Ernest Morrell's speech was given moments before the members of the Council of Youth Research presented their work as part of the American Educational Research Association's annual meeting in Denver, Colorado. In the busy hallway of conference activity, students listened and grounded themselves in the feeling of speculative change. What drives us to transform the world around us and to transform ourselves for this better world? For Ernest and many of us as members of this Council, it is outrage.

How dare this country assume that the present is good enough? And how dare we settle for educational mediocrity, as teachers and as members of this public sphere? And how dare the individuals who chose to attend this session expect to see only young people sharing scholarship that is disconnected from demands for real world change? For Ernest, the fight for transformation is taken up through words. Language and its capacity to pierce the hearts of those around us is the mechanism for voicing and leveraging outrage.

It is in the spirit of this anger and the potent ways it sticks to our ribs that we conclude this book. We, too, are angry. We are not satisfied with pedagogies and policies that act as mere Band-Aids for a desperately flawed world. This book and its commitments are not meant as an act of only repairing the wounds of settler colonial and anti-Black violence that are shaped in schools every day. Rather, these are commitments for the making of a new world.

Flexibility and Teaching for the Future

Throughout this book we've offered the tools for tackling speculative dreaming in our classrooms. These are civic underpinnings for every classroom and the necessary work to support every student. The commitments that we point to throughout this book are intentionally malleable because we don't know what your community's needs are, the challenges your future holds, or the contexts of joyful learning in the days to come. An unspoken and final commitment for speculative dreaming, then, is flexibility.

How will we bend and twist the resources and expectations in front of us into transformational experiences for our students? What we cannot do is diminish the critical purposes of our work—the "why"—that must remain as the foundation. But when we look at a calendar rife with mandated assessments, or a textbook of unimaginative and regressive content, or a set of soul-deadening professional development sessions, how might we look at these requirements and find an iota of joy and creativity within them? This is the flexibility that we must commit to. It will allow us to drive through ongoing approaches to inquiry, imagination, storytelling, networking, and advocacy.

Part of the flexibility that we need to maintain is about the very notion of speculative education. Often, when we imagine science fiction and the powerful stories of Afro- and Latinx-futurists that inspire our work, new technologies and societies in some far away future are depicted. While that is one future, we want to recognize that other futures are always on a graspable horizon. Tomorrow is the future. The moment before you read this next sentence is the future. We must adjust our expectations and demand better conditions for a world to come in future generations and a world to come momentarily. This is a multisighted vision of the future toward which we must work.

Perhaps it may feel counterintuitive, but if we are to hold fast and flexibly to the commitments of this book and to a better world to come, we need to live and work and organize and teach as if the future is always now. We need to feel the present moment—feel the anger—that motivates us as it motivates Morrell, but we need to do so while situating ourselves in the future. This may sound silly or idealistic, but it takes courage and imagination to move and act within the inequitable boundaries of today and transform the world around us to the best of our abilities.

From manifesting principles that intentionally dismantle anti-Blackness within our curriculum to shifting the physical layout of our classroom spaces to create more democratic forms of engagement, we need to make physical, emotional, and intellectual shifts in our work to bring the future into the here and now. This is the speculative living we must embody. It requires imagination and that can be a hard thing to manifest in a sociopolitical context that seeks to stifle the imaginations of young people and teachers alike.

At the time that we write this, the generational impacts of No Child Left Behind (NCLB) and similar high-stakes assessment-driven models of teacher and student performance like Race to the Top and the Every Student Succeeds Act have quietly redefined what we—as a society—think schools are capable of achieving. We have reshaped schools around the assumption that we must march toward end-of-term summative assessments that are driven toward particular forms of knowledge acquisition (e.g., the banking model that Freire has warned us of). There is a double bind in this context. On the one hand, we have made it hard for teachers to imagine an otherwise. At the same time, this is the very system that created the current crop of new teachers. The majority of the preservice teachers that we (coauthors Nicole and

Antero) teach today came of age as youth within models of NCLB-framed educational policy. While it might not be the perfect system in the eyes of these student teachers, they are signing up to teach within this inequitable system.

Breaking out of this model requires looking for ideas in the liminal spaces of literature, daydreams, and storytelling. This book has sought to offer ongoing examples of how we might make these kinds of shifts—in individual and programmatic ways—in the present moment, working toward speculative ends. The past, too, can offer us blueprints for how our systems have sparked alternative means of sustaining teacher and student humanity. Finally, taking on a playful ethos can help reshape what we see as possible today.

Dutch theorist Johan Huizinga (1955) offers the notion of the "magic circle," which has been taken up widely in the area of gaming research. Huizinga recognizes that when people voluntarily enter into a game they are standing "consciously outside 'ordinary' life . . . absorbing the player . . . utterly" (p. 13). Simply, when you play a game, you can step outside the rules and assumptions of what is permissible or even possible. You can become a raging capitalist in Monopoly, a fiendishly hungry hippo in Hungry Hungry Hippos, or a sweets-loving explorer in the world of Candy Land, to name a few familiar examples. Your behavior as a cutthroat competitor, a famished mammal, and an intrepid explorer of a fictitious world allows you to do things that may not be possible in the real world that lives outside the magic circle of the game. More recent scholarship only further affirms the important role that the magic circle plays in gaming contexts (Garcia, 2017; Salen & Zimmerman, 2004).

Here's where the magic circle comes into play in our work as flexible curators of the world of tomorrow. Ask yourself what it would mean to look at the world through the same sense of playfulness that we enter into when we let our guard down and play a game of charades or turn into a dragon to playfully chase a toddler around a backyard. When we enter a world of our making, we make of it what we choose and we must choose freedom.

What would it mean to draw an imaginary circle around your classroom, your school, and your school community and pretend to live the otherwise? Part of the idea behind the Black Cloud game was that pretending to be citizen scientists and collecting data about air pollution or designing ecotopias meant that students actually took on these roles. By entering the magic circle and allowing themselves to take on playful identities, students developed real skills and real awareness of the contexts of hyperlocal environmental change around them. This is the powerful porousness of the magic circle—that by entering a world of pretend you just might be transforming the actual world around you. With this in mind, we need to be even more intentional about the theories of change from which we are operating as we conclude this book.

Theory of Change

It is easy to be dissatisfied with the state of the world. Frankly, there are plenty of reasons to remain furious about the injustices around you, experienced by you and your students, and with which this profession sometimes makes us complicit. From the periods of doom scrolling through horrific atrocities amplified on social media, to witnessing in-person harm, to breathing in the effects of wildfires due to ongoing climate devastation, to internalizing daily microaggressions within your work setting, there are many ways that we exist in a landscape of harm and ignorance. Too often, this profession tells us implicitly and explicitly to set these feelings aside. That good teaching means that even if we care a lot about the world around us, keeping ours and our students' heads down and plowing through content will ultimately make their lives better. We know that's not the case. We cannot turn off the world around us or how it makes us feel.

We also know that, in recent years, our profession has been coming to terms with the social and emotional needs of our students. When they hurt because of a local tragedy in their school community or because of fear of mass shootings in this country or because of climate dread, teachers often foreground these needs and ignore their own emotional well-being in the process (Garcia, 2019).

While it is easy to sit with our dissatisfaction, moving toward action requires imagination and defending that imagination with righteous vigilance. Maybe the action you'll take up has to do with words—like Morrell's. Maybe you will move toward a kind of speculative story-telling that reaches new audiences in new ways. Maybe it's about the day-to-day work that transforms student learning in your classroom. Whatever it is, we want to encourage you now to consider what your personal theory of change is. How do you imagine transformation occurs around you and what role and responsibility do you take in this process?

For example, one reason that we left the high school English class-rooms we spent years working in was a belief in change and trans-formation through teacher-education models—like many of the ideas we've shared in this book. Do we sometimes look back wistfully at the lives we lived previously at our respective high schools? Of course. But we see the political work we do working alongside all of you as a part of a shared theory of change and how we help align all of us in the same march toward freedom.

In addition to articulating your theory of change, you might want to consider the speed of this change and if you are comfortable with it. For example, many theories of change focus on deliberate, incremental change. Small and iterative growth—the groundswell of gaining ever more hearts and minds organized for a shared purpose—takes time, and this theory implies that change will take eons to be fully realized.

While we acknowledge that change takes time and work, we also conclude this book impatient with the present moment and no lon-ger willing to simply wait or vote for better alternatives. We need to act upon theories of change that move at the urgency of humanity. To be clear, imagination is not wielded solely by those aligned in our fight against oppression. If we look at the imaginative civic acts under-taken by proponents of far right political ideologies in recent years, we see actions that have led to rapid and sweeping changes—theories of change that while long in the works take place nearly or even liter-ally overnight. Donald Trump's January 2017 "Muslim ban" executive order, the January 6, 2021 insurrection, and a carefully constructed Supreme Court that overturned *Roe v. Wade*—these are all forms of harmful civic change that came into effect very quickly, even if the seeds for such insidious change were planted long before. If transformation can occur to produce harmful outcomes at a rapid pace, might we—we who are aligned for collective peace—also sprint into faster action?

We are reminded of water's transformation into ice. A single degree of cooling turns a liquid into a solid. There is no in-between. One moment, water splashes and resists definition. The next it is brittle and sharp. That instantaneous transformation from one thing into another—that is an enunciation of a kind of change we might be able to manifest in our classrooms and with students, teachers, families, and community members.

Planning and deliberate action require care. We are not advocating recklessly jumping into situations without making full sense of the contexts and risks. Rather, we want to urge you to remember that while change often is slow, it does not have to be. We do not have to accept that the world we are striving for is destined for someone else's lifetime. We write of the shared civic commitments in this book because we fully intend to celebrate the fruits of our shared efforts alongside you and to do so soon. Like our move from K–12 classrooms into our roles as researchers and educators in higher education, this book is an act of seed spreading and working to help grow alongside all of you.

Finally, we want to recall that these theories of change and these commitments in this book are never fixed in place. Social movements move. What might have been nonnegotiable commitments at the time that we write this book might require reinterrogation and innovation. Just as every chapter of this book looked at the sometimes-flawed histories of civic action in our classrooms, we must give ourselves permission to shift, to change our minds, and to push beyond the imagination of the present moment. By the time you read these words they have aged. We hope they maintain utility for our profession for some time, but there will likely be a period where you will need to push beyond the ideas shared here. The present moment demands your presence and it demands continually reinventing what we do.

Marching Orders

As students, teachers, and researchers prepared to share their work together as the Council of Youth Research, Ernest Morrell reminded us all that these presentations were so much more than just a show-and-tell. If words beget action as one theory of change, then each time the Council presented was an opportunity to recruit new members into our social movement, a new opportunity to further social progress, a new opportunity to build for the world of tomorrow alongside the individuals in the room. In this way, Morrell would remind everyone: Do not let a single person leave the room without knowing their marching orders. What is it that the Council wants people to do? How do we want them to act based on what we share?

These marching orders—and the need to write and communicate them—have been an animating beacon for how we have thought about our work as teacher educators and educational researchers. It is not enough to simply articulate new modes of knowledge or to teach the latest pedagogical innovations to a new generation of educators. Rather, these are political acts. We willfully imbue this profession with civic expectations through how and where we share our research and how we work to teach new teachers. We end our research articles with deliberate calls for action for our academic colleagues and we end our classes with marching orders for our teachers. So, in this spirit, we conclude this book with a set of marching orders for you, for our colleagues who may not have read this book yet, and for us as a collective wanting more than what this educational world has offered so far.

Remember and embrace the feeling of being creative and empowered. This is a profession that is built on our ingenuity and expertise. Various stakeholders over the past several decades have done their best to infantilize the teaching profession and to offer as scripted a curriculum as possible in an attempt to control student learning and wrest it out of the hands of attentive and caring teachers. We need to recognize that teachers and students are the experts in the present moment and know the needs and pedagogical approaches that align with what's happening in their own classrooms.

Publicly celebrate yourself and the work you are doing. If you take up any of the civic commitments in this book, demonstrate the shifts in your work. When you see growth in your practice or new insights from your students, amplify these phenomena and celebrate them. Let others—in your school and in your online social networks—see what you are doing. This demonstration is a form of its own kind of social transformation.

Do not settle for tepid compromises when it comes to equity. Too often, our activist approaches are met with shrugged shoulders and tepid shifts. "Of course we'd like to improve the learning outcomes for our historically marginalized youth of color," one administrator might say, "but it's out of my hands." We must be steadfast in our demands for change. When things begin to bend toward us, do not imagine the scraps of diversity, equity, and inclusion rhetoric can fully sate the maw of white supremacy. If we are to dismantle the apparatuses of harm in and around schooling systems, we cannot settle for the smallest amounts of change.

Expand the civic possibilities around you. Our speculative vision of civics in this book demands that we do not stick with the systems and strategies that presently exist. While we believe in the power of the ballot, we are also reminded that the voting decisions in this country cannot extricate us from (and have sometimes led us to) the civic quagmire in which we presently find ourselves. Look for ways to expand the civic opportunities and innovations of the students around you. Above all, remain intolerant of work that does not see our students as fully human.

Lastly, find rest. The narratives of self-care, as we discussed earlier in this book, are harmful in the ways they ignore the systemic conditions that burden us daily. And yet, we affirm that rest is a necessary force for change and for good. It is the act of insurgency Audre Lorde called for in her poetry.

These have been restless years for generations of teachers and students. Anxiety, loss, dehumanization, and violence have all crowded the passages of time through which we weather. This restlessness fosters an agitation to want to act upon the system and attempt to do something more than maintain the stasis of educational mediocrity in which we've been absorbed. It also implies that we have been without rest throughout this time. We are simultaneously awaiting eagerly an otherwise and exhausted by the harsh state of the schooling system. To know rest and to be able to rest: that would mean we've found freedom in our collective, speculative journeys. It would mean finding wholeness through our shared civic commitments.

Coda

At the end of the first school year of the 3D Project, we noticed that even as students demonstrated curiosity and creativity in their imaginings about possible civic futures, they continued to harbor a substantial amount of doubt about the willingness of the wider public to engage in the same practices of dreaming they did. When the teachers asked all of the students in the project to quantify their feelings about the possibility of people in the United States being able to dialogue productively about controversial social issues in their lifetimes, with 1 being extremely pessimistic and 4 being extremely optimistic, the great majority of students (186 out of 228) found themselves in the 2–3 range. Their accompanying open responses indicated their uneasiness about the tenor of today's public dialogue and the extent to which individuals are actually willing to empathize across lines of difference. Heather from California wrote, "I don't believe people in this day and age are mature enough to handle talking about things they disagree about without fighting or arguing as is often shown in our political system." Sixty-eight percent of open responses referenced dialogue as devolving into arguments or name-calling.

Yet, in a rumination on the pull between futurist and pessimist perspectives, students also offered tentative gestures of hope. Ana from Texas wrote, "I think our generation is growing to have better conversations." The act of future making is not work that necessarily has clear, measurable, and standards-aligned goals. The speculative optimism and pessimism that students voiced throughout this project bring to light that youth leading requires pedagogic support in classrooms and will require constant reflection, reevaluation, and revision. As Tara from Michigan wrote, "I'd like to be optimistic and think people will evolve." Monica from Pennsylvania wrote: "I hesitate but I do have hope." We believe that this combination of hesitation and hope speaks volumes about our current moment—and what all of us who educate can take with us on the journey ahead.

References

Anderson, J. [James Anderson]. (2014, February 16). Angela Davis talk at SIUC on Feb. 13, 2014 [Video]. YouTube. https://www.youtube .com/watch?v=6s8QCucFADc

Anyon, J. (1980). Social class and the hidden curriculum of work. *Journal of Education, 162*(1), 67–92.

Anzaldúa, G. (1987). Borderlands/La frontera: The new mestiza. Aunt Lute Books.

Au, W. (2009). *Unequal by design: High-stakes testing and the standardization of inequality.* Routledge.

Baker, E. (1969). *The black woman in the civil rights struggle* [Speech]. Institute for the Black World, Atlanta, GA. Accessed from https:// repository.duke.edu/dc/holsaertfaith/fhpst05001

Banks, J. (2017). Failed citizenship and transformative civic education. *Educational Researcher, 46*(7), 366–377.

Bartels, L. (2018). *Unequal democracy: The political economy of the new gilded age* (2nd ed.). Princeton University Press.

Benjamin, R. (2017). "But . . . there are new suns!" *Palimpsest: A Journal on Women, Gender, and the Black International, 6*(2), 103–105.

Boardman, A., Garcia, A., & Dalton, B. (2021). *Compose our world: Engaging educators and students with project-based learning in secondary English language arts.* Teachers College Press.

Boellstorff, T. (2008). Coming of age in Second Life: An anthropologist explores the virtually human. Princeton University Press.

Booth, S. E., & Kellogg, S. B. (2015). Value creation in online communities for educators. *British Journal of Educational Technology, 46*, 684–698.

Bourdieu, P. (1985). The forms of capital. In J. Richardson (Ed.), *Handbook of theory and research for the sociology of education* (pp. 241–258). Greenwood.

Boyte, H. (2003). A different kind of politics: John Dewey and the meaning of citizenship in the 21st century. *The Good Society, 12*(2), 1–15.

Brooklyn Academy of Music. [BAMorg]. (2019, October 21). *N. K. Jemisin and Ijeoma Oluo on activism as a creative practice* [Video]. YouTube. https://www.youtube.com/watch?v=456smnRWb_4

brown, a. m. (2017). *Emergent strategy: Shaping change, changing worlds.* AK Press.

Camangian, P. (2010). Starting with self: Teaching autoethnography to foster critically caring literacies. *Research in the Teaching of English 45*(2), 179–204.

Cammarota, J., & Fine, M. (2008). *Revolutionizing education: Youth participatory action research in motion.* Routledge.

Cammarota, J., & Romero, A. (2011). Participatory action research for high school students: Transforming policy, practice, and the personal with social justice education. *Educational Policy, 25*, 488–506.

Caraballo, L., Lozenski, B., Lyiscott, J., & Morrell, E. (2017). YPAR and critical epistemologies: Rethinking education research. *Review of Research in Education, 41*(1), 311–336.Chen, M. (2011*). Leet noobs: The life and death of an expert player group in World of Warcraft.* Peter Lang.

Coates, T. (2015). *Between the world and me.* Random House.

Cochran-Smith, M., & Lytle, S. L. (2009). *Inquiry as stance: Practitioner research for a new generation.* Teachers College Press.

Cohen, C., Kahne, J., & Marshall, J. (2018). Let's go there: Race, ethnicity and a lived civics approach to civics education. GenForward, University of Chicago. https://www.civicsurvey.org/publications/lets-go-there

Cohen, C., Kahne, J., Bowyer, B., Middaugh, E., & Rogowski, J. (2012). Participatory politics: New media and youth political action. Youth and Participatory Politics Research Network. https://

ypp.dmlcentral.net/sites/default/files/publications/Participatory_
Politics_New_Media_and_Youth_Political_Action.2012.pdf

Cortez, A., McKoy, A., & Lizárraga, J. R. (2022). The future of young Blacktivism: Aesthetics and practices of speculative activism in video game play. *The Journal of Futures Studies, 26*(3) 53-70.

Crenshaw, K., Gotanda, N., Peller, G., & Thomas, K. (Eds). (1995). *Critical race theory: The key writings that formed the movement.* New Press.

Cuauhtin, R., Zavala, M., Sleeter, C., & Au, W. (2019). *Rethinking ethnic studies.* Rethinking Schools.

Cushman, K. (1997). Making the whole student visible: The descriptive review of a child. Horace, 13(2), 7. Accessed from http://essentialschools.org/horace-issues/making-the-whole-student-visible-the-descriptive-review-of-a-child/

Davis, N. R., & Schaeffer, J. (2019). Troubling troubled waters in elementary science education: Politics, ethics and black children's conceptions of water justice in the era of Flint. *Cognition and Instruction, 37*(3), 367–389.

Dewey, J. (1916). *Democracy and education: An introduction to the philosophy of education.* Macmillan.

Didion, J. (2006). *We tell ourselves stories in order to live: Collected nonfiction.* Everyman's Library.

Dillon, G. (Ed.). (2012). *Walking the clouds: An anthology of indigenous science fiction.* University of Arizona Press.

Du Bois, W. E. B. (1903). *The souls of black folk.* Modern World Library.

Duncan-Andrade, J. M. R., & Morrell, E. (2008). *The art of critical pedagogy: Possibilities for moving from theory to practice in urban schools.* Peter Lang.

Ebarvia, T., Germán, L., Parker, K. & Torres, J. (2020). #DisruptTexts: An introduction. *English Journal, 110*(1), 100–102.

Eco, U. (2006). *The island of the day before.* HarperVia.

Emdin, C. (2016). *For white folks who teach in the hood . . . and the rest of y'all, too: Reality pedagogy and urban education.* Beacon Press.

Fleischer, C., & Garcia, A. (2020). *Everyday advocacy for literacy educators: Teachers find a voice, take a stand, change the narrative.* Norton.

Freire, P. (1970). *Pedagogy of the oppressed.* Seabury Press.

Freire, P. (2005). *Teachers as cultural workers: Letters to those who dare teach* (expanded ed.). Westview Press.

Ganz, M. (2011). Public Narrative, Collective Action, and Power. In Odugbemi, S. & Lee, T. (Eds.), *Accountability Through Public Opinion: From Inertia to Public Action* (pp. 273–289). Washington DC: The World.

Garcia, A. (2017). *Good reception: Teens, teachers, and mobile media in a Los Angeles high school.* MIT Press.

Garcia, A. (2019). A call for healing teachers: Loss, ideological unravelling, and the healing gap. *Schools: Studies in Education, 16*(1), 64–83.

Garcia, A., & Morrell, E. (2022). *Tuned-in teaching: Centering youth culture for an active and just classroom.* Heinemann.

Ginwright, S., & Cammarota, J. (2007) Youth activism in the urban community: Learning critical civic praxis within community organizations. *International Journal of Qualitative Studies in Education, 20,* 693–710.

Ginwright, S., Noguera, P., & Cammarota, J. (Eds.). (2006). *Beyond resistance! Youth activism and community change: New democratic possibilities for practice and policy for America's youth.* Routledge.

Glaude, E. (2007). *In a shade of blue: Pragmatism and the politics of black America.* University of Chicago Press.

Gould, J. (2011). Guardian of democracy: The civic mission of schools. Leonore Annenberg Institute for Civics of the Annenberg Public Policy Center at the University of Pennsylvania. https://www.carnegie.org/publications/guardianof-democracy-the-civic-mission-of-schools/

Greene, M. (2000). *Releasing the imagination: Essays on education, the arts, and social change.* Jossey-Bass.

Gutiérrez, K. D. (2008). Developing a sociocritical literacy in the third space. *Reading Research Quarterly, 43*(2), 148–164.

Hannah-Jones, N. (2021). *The 1619 project: A new origin story.* One World.

Hartman, S. (2019). *Wayward lives, beautiful experiments: Intimate histories of riotous Black girls, troublesome women, and queer radicals.* Norton.

Hellekson, K., and Busse, K. (2014). *The Fan Fiction Studies Reader.* University of Iowa Press.

Hess, D., & McAvoy, P. (2016). *The political classroom: Evidence and ethics in democratic education.* Routledge.

Huizinga, J. (1955). *Homo ludens: A study of the play-element in culture.* Beacon Press.

Imarisha, W. (2015). Introduction. In W. Imarisha & a.m. brown (Eds.), Octavia's brood: Science fiction stories from social justice movements (pp. 3-6). AK Press.

Irizarry, J. (2009). Reinvigorating multicultural education through youth participatory action research. *Multicultural Perspectives, 11*, 194–199.

Ito, M., Gutiérrez, K., Livingstone, S., Penuel, B., Rhodes, J., Salen, K., . . . Craig Watkins, S. (2013). *Connected learning: An agenda for research and design.* Digital Media and Learning Research Hub.

Jenkins, H., Clinton, K., Purushotma, R., Robison, A. J., & Weigel, M. (2009). *Confronting the challenges of participatory culture: Media education for the 21st century.* MacArthur Foundation.

Jenkins, H., Ito, M., & boyd, d. (2015). *Participatory culture in a networked era.* Polity.

Jenkins, H., Peters-Lazaro, G., & Shresthova, S. (2020). *Popular culture and the civic imagination: Case studies of creative social change.* New York University Press.

Jenkins, H., Shresthova, S., Gamber-Thompson, L., Kliger-Vilenchik, N., & Zimmerman, A. (2016). *By any media necessary: The new youth activism.* New York University Press.

Kahne, J., & Bowyer, B. (2017). Educating for democracy in a partisan age: Confronting the challenges of motivated reasoning and misinformation. *American Educational Research Journal, 54*(1), 3–34.

Kelly, L. (2020). Listening differently: Youth self-actualization through critical Hip Hop literacies. *English Teaching: Practice & Critique, 19*(3), 269–285.

Kennedy, R. F. (1968, March 18). Remarks at the University of Kansas. Accessed from https://www.jfklibrary.org/learn/about-jfk/the-kennedy-family/robert-f-kennedy/robert-f-kennedy-speeches/remarks-at-the-university-of-kansas-march-18-1968

Kirshner, B. (2015). *Youth activism in an era of education inequality.* New York University Press.

Kokka, K. (2019). Healing-informed social justice mathematics: Promoting students' sociopolitical consciousness and well-being in mathematics class. *Urban Education, 54*(9), 1179–1209.

Krashen, S. D. (2004). *The power of reading: Insights from the research* (2nd ed.). Libraries Unlimited, Heinemann.

Kwon, L., & de los Ríos, C. V. (2019). "See, click, fix": Civic interrogation and digital tools in a ninth-grade ethnic studies course. *Equity & Excellence in Education, 52*(2–3), 154–166. https://doi.org/10.1080/10665684.2019.1647809

Lee, C. D., White, G., & Dong, D. (Eds.). (2021). *Educating for civic reasoning and discourse.* National Academy of Education.

Lee, C., Meltzoff, A. & Kuhl, P. (2020). The braid of human learning and development: Neuro-physiological processes and participation in cultural practices. In N.A. Nasir, C. Lee, R. Pea, M. McKinney de Royston (Eds.), *Handbook of the cultural foundations of learning* (pp. 24–43). Routledge.

Lo, J. C. (2019). The role of civic debt in democratic education. *Multicultural Perspectives, 21*(2), 112–118.

Mar, R., & Oatley, K. (2008). The function of fiction is the abstraction and simulation of social experience. *Perspectives on Psychological Science, 3*(3), 173–192.

Miller, D. (2009). *The book whisperer: Awakening the inner reader in every child* (1st ed.). Jossey-Bass.

Mirra, N. (2018). *Educating for empathy: Literacy learning and civic engagement.* Teachers College Press.

Mirra, N., & Garcia, A. (2022). Guns, schools, and democracy: Adolescents imagining social futures through speculative civic literacies. *American Educational Research Journal, 59*(2), 345–380.

Mirra, N., & Garcia, A. (2017). Civic participation re-imagined: Youth interrogation and innovation in the multimodal public sphere. *Review of Research in Education, 41*(1), 136–158.

Mirra, N., Garcia, A., & Morrell, E. (2015). *Doing youth participatory action research: Transforming inequity with researchers, educators, and youth.* Routledge.

Moll, L., Amanti, C., Neff, D., & Gonzalez, N. (1992). Funds of knowledge for teaching: Using a qualitative approach to connect homes and classrooms. *Theory Into Practice, 31*, 132–141.

Morrell, E. (2008). *Critical literacy and urban youth: Pedagogies of access, dissent and liberation*. Routledge.

Nardi, B. (2010). *My life as a night elf priest: An anthropological account of World of Warcraft*. University of Michigan Press.

Nasir, N., Lee, C., Pea, R., & McKinney de Royston, M. (2021). Rethinking learning: What the interdisciplinary science tells us. *Educational Researcher, 50*(8), 557– 565.

National Assessment of Educational Progress [NAEP] Civics Project. (2014). *Civics framework for the 2014 National Assessment of Educational Progress*. National Assessment Governing Board.

National Governors Association. (2010). *Common Core State Standards for English Language Arts & Literacy in History/Social Studies*.

NCTE Task Force on Assessment. (2013). *Formative assessment that truly informs instruction*. National Council of Teachers of English.

Nieto, S., & Bode, P. (2008). *Affirming diversity: The sociopolitical context of multicultural education* (5th ed.). Allyn & Bacon.

Otieno Sumba, E. (2018, October 22). The Black speculative arts movement and Afrofuturism as an Afrocentric, technocultural social philosophy. *Griot*. https://griotmag.com/ en/the-black-speculative-arts-movement-afrofuturism-as-an-afrocentric-technocultural-social-philosophy/

Ozer, E. J., Ritterman, M. L., & Wanis, M. G. (2010). Participatory action research (Par) in middle school: Opportunities, constraints, and key processes. *American Journal of Community Psychology, 46*(1–2), 152–166.

Pearce, C., & Artemesia. (2009). Communities of play: Emergent cultures in multiplayer games and virtual worlds. MIT Press.

Peters-Lazaro, G., & Shresthova, S. (2020). *Practicing futures: A civic imagination action handbook*. Peter Lang.

Pfister, R. C. (2014). *Hats for house elves: Connected learning and civic engagement in Hogwarts at Ravelry*. Irvine, CA: Digital Media and Learning Research Hub.

Philip, T. M., & Garcia, A. (2015). Schooling mobile phones: Assumptions about proximal benefits, the challenges of shifting meanings, and the politics of teaching. *Educational Policy, 29*(4), 676–707.

Polman, J. L. (2012). Trajectories of participation and identification in learning communities involving disciplinary practices. In D. Yun Dai (Ed.), *Design research on learning and thinking in educational settings: Enhancing intellectual growth and functioning* (pp. 225-242). New York: Routledge.

Rafalow, M. H., & Tekinbas, K. S. (2014). *Welcome to Sackboy Planet: Connected learning among LittleBigPlanet 2 players.* Irvine, CA: Digital Media and Learning Research Hub.

Ransby, B. (2005). *Ella Baker and the Black freedom movement: A radical democratic vision.* University of North Carolina Press.

Richardson, L. (1994). Writing: A method of inquiry. In N. K. Denzin, Y. S. Lincoln (Eds.), *Handbook of qualitative research* (pp. 516–529). Sage.

Salen, K., & Zimmerman, E. (2004). *Rules of play: Game design fundamentals.* MIT Press.

Shapiro, S., & Brown, C. (2018, Summer). A look at civics education in the United States. *American Educator.*

Solorzano, D., & Delgado-Bernal, D. (2001). Examining transformational resistance through a critical race and LatCrit theory framework: Chicana and Chicano students in an urban context. *Urban Education, 36,* 308–342.

Spires, D. (2019). *The practice of citizenship: Black politics and print culture in the early United States.* University of Pennsylvania Press.

Standage, T. (1998). *The Victorian Internet: The remarkable story of the telegraph and the nineteenth century's on-line pioneers.* Walker and Co.

T F. [T F]. (2012, March 3). *David Coleman, 'Bringing the common core to life'* [Video]. YouTube. https://www.youtube.com/watch?v=Pu6lin88YXU

Thomas, E. E., & Stornaiuolo, A. (2016). Restorying the self: Bending toward textual justice. *Harvard Educational Review, 86*(3), 313–338.

Timberg, C. (2021). New whistleblower claims Facebook allowed hate, illegal activity to go unchecked. *Washington Post.* Retrieved from https://www.washingtonpost.com/technology/2021/10/22/facebook-new-whistleblower-complaint/

Tippett, K. (2022). The grounding virtues of the On Being Project. The On Being Project. https://onbeing.org/social-healing-at-on-being/the-six-grounding-virtues-of-the-on-being-project/

Torney-Purta, J., & Vermeer, S. (2006). *Developing citizenship competencies from kindergarten through Grade 12: A background paper for policymakers and educators.* Education Commission of the States.

Tyack, D., & Cuban, L. (1997). *Tinkering toward utopia: A century of public school reform.* Harvard University Press.

Valenzuela, A. (1999). *Subtractive schooling: U.S.-Mexican youth and the politics of caring.* SUNY Press.

Vickery, A. (2017). "You excluded us for so long and now you want us to be patriotic?" African American women teachers navigating the quandary of citizenship. *Theory & Research in Social Education, 45*(3), 318–348.

Watts, R., Diemer, M. A., & Voight, A. M. (2011). Critical consciousness: Current status and future directions. *New Directions for Child and Adolescent Development, 134,* 43–57.

Watts, R., & Flanagan, C. (2007). Pushing the envelope on civic engagement: A developmental and liberation psychology perspective. *Journal of Community Psychology, 35*(6), 779–792.

Watts, R., & Hipolito-Delgado, C. (2015). Thinking ourselves to liberation? Advancing sociopolitical action in critical consciousness. *Urban Review, 47,* 847–867.

Westheimer, J., & Kahne, J. (2004). What kind of citizen? The politics of educating for democracy. *American Educational Research Journal, 41,* 237–269.

Wiggington, E. (Ed.). (1968). *The Foxfire book.* Anchor Books.

Wolff, J. (2016). *An introduction to political philosophy* (3rd ed.). Oxford University Press.

Yang, K. W. (2009). Mathematics, critical literacy, and youth participatory action research. *New Directions for Youth Development, 123,* 99–118.

Youniss, J. (2011). Civic education: What schools can do to

encourage civic identity and action. *Applied Developmental Science,* *15*(2), 98–103.

Yosso, T. (2005a). *Critical race counterstories along the Chicana/Chicano educational pipeline.* Routledge.

Yosso, T. (2005b). Whose culture has capital? A critical race theory discussion of community cultural wealth. *Race, Ethnicity and Education, 8,* 69–91.

Zadbood, A., Chen, J., Leong, Y.C., Norman, K.A. & Hasson, U. (2017). How we transmit memories to other brains: Constructing shared neural representations via communication. *Cerebral Cortex, 27*(10), 4988–5000.

Index

About the Authors

Nicole Mirra is an associate professor of urban teacher education in the Graduate School of Education at Rutgers University. She previously taught secondary literacy and debate in Brooklyn, New York and Los Angeles, California. Her research utilizes participatory design methods in classrooms, communities, and digital spaces to create civic learning environments with youth and educators that disrupt discourses and structures of racial injustice and creatively compose liberatory social futures. Her previous books include *Educating for Empathy: Literacy Learning and Civic Engagement* (Teachers College Press, 2018) and *Doing Youth Participatory Action Research: Transforming Inquiry with Researchers, Educators, and Students* (Routledge, 2015).

Antero Garcia is an associate professor in the Graduate School of Education at Stanford University. Prior to completing his PhD, Antero was an English teacher at a public high school in South Central Los Angeles. His research explores the possibilities of speculative imagination and healing in educational research. Based on this research, Antero codesigned the Critical Design and Gaming School—a public high school in Los Angeles. He has authored or edited more than a dozen books about the possibilities of literacies, play, and civics in transforming schooling in the United States.